Ramps & Pathways

A Constructivist Approach to
Physics with Young Children

Rheta DeVries and Christina Sales

National Association for the Education of Young Children

Washington, DC

National Association
for the Education
of Young Children
1313 L Street NW, Suite 500
Washington, DC 20005-4101
202-232-8777 • 800-424-2460
www.naeyc.org

NAEYC Books
Editor in Chief
Akimi Gibson

Editorial Director
Bry Pollack

Design and Production
Malini Dominey

Editorial Associate
Melissa Hogarty

Editorial Assistant
Elizabeth Wegner

Permissions
Lacy Thompson

Through its publications program, the National Association for the Education of Young Children (NAEYC) provides a forum for discussion of major issues and ideas in the early childhood field, with the hope of provoking thought and promoting professional growth. The views expressed or implied in this book are not necessarily those of the Association or its members.

Credits: Photographs copyright © by: *Malini Dominey*, 8–9, 94; *Regents' Center for Early Developmental Education*, viii, 13, 17, 27, 33, 42–43, 46–47, 49–52, 55–63, 71, 73, 76, 85, 88–89, 97–98, back cover; *Lydia Christine Sales*, vii; *Lloyd Wolf*, cover, 10, 22, 36, 64

Acknowledgments: Peggy Ashbrook, preschool science teacher and columnist for *Science and Children*, National Science Teachers Association, for providing the resources on page 78

For more resources on Ramps & Pathways, visit www.naeyc.org

Library of Congress Control Number: 2010935436

ISBN: 978-1-928896-69-2

NAEYC Item #352

To know an object is to act upon it and to transform it . . .

—Jean Piaget, *Science of Education and the Psychology of the Child*

What is desired is that the teacher cease being a lecturer, satisfied with transmitting ready-made solutions; his role should rather be that of a mentor stimulating initiative and research.

—Jean Piaget, *To Understand Is to Invent*

Contents

Acknowledgments

We would like to thank so many people that our task is impossible. Our debt is first of all to the children and teachers of Freeburg School, which was operated for six years by the Regents' Center for Early Developmental Education at the University of Northern Iowa (faculty and staff listed below) when Rheta was the director of the Regents' Center.

We thank Dr. Thomas Switzer, Dean of the College of Education, for the original dream of building a school. It was at Freeburg School that teachers' and children's work convinced us that Ramps & Pathways activities had special value for children's learning and development. Freeburg teachers and other staff members, members of our Teacher Practitioner Councils, teachers who were participants in a National Science Foundation pilot project, and Regents' Center Fellows and staff contributed by sharing their experimentation, participating in discussions, and providing feedback on an early draft of this book. Technical staff of the Regents' Center worked to search our video and photographic archives for examples to illustrate our text. Photographs were taken mainly by teachers and audiovisual specialists. We also want to thank our secretary, Theresa Johnson, and our clerk, Cathy Pearson.

We are indebted to the U.S. Department of Education for Grants R215K010030 and U215K032257, supporting work that led to a first draft, and to the National Science Foundation Grant, Ramps and Pathways: A Constructivist Approach to Teaching Physical Science, DRL-0628082, that supported a revision.

Our thanks are also due to Dr. Constance Kamii for critical feedback on an earlier draft. Special thanks go to Sharon Doolittle, who brought to us the idea of using cove molding as Ramps & Pathways. On a personal note we thank Jeffry Sales for his support throughout the writing of this book.

Fellows of the Regents' Center for Early Developmental Education
Dr. Rebecca Edmiaston
Dr. Judy Finkelstein
Dr. Linda May Fitzgerald
Dr. Carolyn Hildebrandt
Dr. Jill Uhlenberg
Dr. Betty Zan

Research Associates
Kathy Thompson
Sonia Yoshizawa
Rosemary Geiken
Secretary: Theresa Johnson

Director of Freeburg School
Jeffry Sales

Freeburg School Faculty
Melissa Anderson
Shirley Bruce
Gloria Galloway
Sherice Hetrick-Ortman
Shari McGhee
Gwen Harmon
Marilyn Luttinen
Beth Van Meeteren
Jane Pearce
Sherri Peterson
Annie Philips
Dr. Annette Swann
Nurse: Jennifer Ritland

Head Start Family Worker
Shelia Woods

Graduate Students
Dr. Seon Chun
Dr. Peter Koech

Audiovisual Specialists
Catherine Richey
Seth Vickers
Clerk: Cathy Pearson

Others who supported the development of Freeburg School and this book:
Donors to the Construction Fund for Freeburg School
Senator Tom Harkin
Senator Charles Grassley
Congressman Jim Nussle
Dr. Lim Kwak
Dr. Yuko Hashimoto

About the Authors

Rheta DeVries retired as professor of curriculum and instruction at the University of Northern Iowa (UNI), where, as director of the Regents' Center for Early Developmental Education, she led the effort to build and develop Freeburg School, a demonstration school for constructivist education. Previously, she held faculty positions at the University of Houston, the Merrill-Palmer Institute, and the University of Illinois at Chicago. DeVries has received many awards, including for significant contribution to the application of constructivist principles in education from the American Educational Research Association (AERA), and for outstanding faculty research from UNI and the University of Houston. Her eight books include *Developing Constructivist Curriculum in Early Education: Practical Principles and Activities* (Teachers College Press, 2002) and *Moral Classrooms, Moral Children: Creating a Constructivist Atmosphere in Early Education* (Teachers College Press, 1994). She received a PhD in psychology from the University of Chicago, and was a postdoctoral fellow of the National Institute of Mental Health for work and study at the University of Geneva, Switzerland.

Christina Sales, an assistant professor at the University of Northern Iowa (UNI), taught young children for more than 20 years. At UNI, she helped establish Freeburg School, where she served as a teacher and curriculum coordinator. Sales has made numerous presentations throughout the world on the education of young children, and is a coauthor of the book *Developing Constructivist Early Childhood Curriculum: Practical Principles and Activities* (Teachers College Press, 2002). Her current focus is working with classroom teachers, developing constructivist early childhood curriculum, and conducting research on early childhood activities. She received an EdD in curriculum and instruction from UNI.

1
Her teacher's respect for Erica's (incorrect) idea about what makes gravel move encourages her to feel confident in her ability to think and experiment.

"Can I Have Your Shovel?"

During outdoor time, 4-year-old Erica was using a shovel to dump pea gravel onto a long, somewhat inclined plastic rain gutter. The gravel hardly moved. Her teacher, Sharon Doolittle, was beside her, shoveling pea gravel onto a shorter, thus more steeply inclined, gutter.

Erica saw Sharon's gravel quickly and noisily skitter down the slope and wanted to produce this interesting result herself. She said to Sharon, "Can I have your shovel?" and Sharon gave it to her. Erica expectantly used the shovel to dump gravel onto her gutter, with the same uninteresting result as before.

In the meantime, Sharon got another shovel and resumed pouring gravel onto her gutter. Again, the gravel skittered down the steep slope. Erica looked surprised, paused, eyed Sharon's new shovel, and again asked, "Can I have your shovel?"

We smile at Erica's idea that using the teacher's shovel would make Erica's gravel move faster down the ramp. No one had taught her this scientifically incorrect idea. Therefore, it must be a product of Erica's own original, spontaneous thinking.

We all have observed such thinking by young children. Occasions such as this often become part of family lore. For example, Rheta's relatives delighted in

1

Should an idea be "wrong"?

Among physical science educators, debate about whether to attribute "misconceptions" or "incorrect ideas" to older children and adults has led some to urge that these terms be abandoned altogether in favor of others such as "preconceptions" or "naïve ideas."

It seems to us that this is a laudable effort to avoid insulting or discouraging those who are trying to understand but whose thinking is scientifically incorrect. We agree with this sensitivity to the feelings of science students and teacher educators.

In this book, however, we are choosing to follow Piaget by writing in terms of young children's "erroneous," "wrong," and "incorrect" ideas about science phenomena. We do not, of course, use these terms with children. In fact, we are not telling children they are right or wrong. Rather, we carefully choose science phenomena and activities so children can test and find out on their own whether their ideas are correct or not.

telling the story of a family trip to Diamond Cave in Arkansas. The low ceilings in the cavern obliged the adults to walk bent over. Everyone laughed when 3-year-old Rheta bent over, too! In the Sales family, a favorite story is about 2-year-old Matthew, excited about a vacation during which they were going to hike. Upon arrival at Rocky Mountain National Park, however, parents Christina and Jeffry were puzzled when Matthew asked, "Where's the football?" Eventually they realized that all Matthew knew about a "hike" was what he had learned playing football with his father!

Like young Rheta and Matthew, all children use what they already have learned and what they observe in the course of figuring out how things work to draw conclusions that we adults—with our greater knowledge and experience—know to be incorrect or misunderstandings. Erica, in trying to figure out a problem she encountered in her physical world, concluded that shovels affect how gravel moves. Rheta, observing the behavior of the adults, concluded that caverns call for walking bent over. Matthew, with his limited verbal knowledge, concluded he would be playing his favorite sport on vacation.

Of course, we want children to acquire correct knowledge and be able to use it. Yet we cannot ignore children's many misconceptions. Erroneous ideas are important because a child's own particular wrong ideas are necessary for that child to reach certain correct ideas. All of us, children or adults, know better and more solidly what is correct when we also know what is *not* correct.

Different children form different wrong ideas. Teachers who respect children's efforts to understand their experiences with physical objects can intervene in ways that create possibilities for children to correct some misconceptions. When children observe physical phenomena that contradict their misconceptions, they have the opportunity to begin to change their ideas. Noting Erica's interest, her teacher offered more activities with inclines in the classroom. These gave Erica the opportunity to experiment, think more deeply about moving objects down inclines, and eventually transform her thinking to include an understanding of the effect that slope has on how gravel moves.

Had Sharon merely shown or told Erica how to arrange her gutter, Erica would have been robbed of the critically important opportunity to figure it out herself. She certainly would not have understood why a steeply sloped gutter works better had her teacher just instructed her on what to do. If Sharon had laughed openly at Erica's amusing idea about shovels, Erica might have felt self-conscious and embarrassed, just as young Rheta remembers feeling in Diamond Cave when she did not understand why everyone laughed at her. If her teacher had told Erica the shovel would not work or had solved the problem for her, Erica's confidence in her ability to think might have been shaken. Instead of reacting in these ways, Sharon respected Erica's shovel idea and cooperated with her in trying it out so that Erica could see for herself that her incorrect idea did not work. We all are more likely to be open to other possibilities when we discover for ourselves that our ideas are incorrect.

Certainly, some knowledge is appropriately taught by telling. Matthew, for example, corrects his misunderstanding once his parents explain that *hike* has several meanings. But as constructivists, we believe knowledge of the physical world is best learned through direct experiences in which children, like Erica, can form ideas, try them out, watch the results, revise their ideas, try them again, and so on. Most of the physical science curricula used in early childhood classrooms include some sort of "hands-on" activity. However, few are designed to engage children deeply in reasoning about physical objects and phenomena in this way—that is, by children experimenting to try out their own ideas. Frequently, too, science topics are limited to a specific age level, with no time allowed for revisiting those topics at a later age.

By contrast, Ramps & Pathways activities are designed for use across a wide range of ages and developmental levels. In this book, we describe how teachers can lead children to construct ever-deepening practical understanding of force and motion, even over several years. We describe what developmental psychologist Jean Piaget called the "roundabout ways" children have shown they must go through in figuring out scientific truths.

Constructivists believe that children "construct" their understanding of the world through a dynamic process of creating, testing, and refining their own ideas about how things work.

The story of "Ramps & Pathways"

This book has its roots in the effort to mine Piaget's research and theory about how children learn and develop for its implications regarding teaching practices. The Ramps & Pathways story begins in the 1970s with work by Rheta in collaboration with Constance Kamii and teachers at the University of Illinois at Chicago's Child Care Center. We drew from Piaget's work the idea of *physical-knowledge* activities as those in which children experiment with objects and object phenomena. One of the many activities we experimented with in the classroom and wrote about in our book *Physical Knowledge in Preschool Education: Implications of Piaget's Theory* (Kamii & DeVries 1978/1993) was called Inclines.

This work inspired Christina in the early 1990s to experiment with physical-knowledge activities in her Plainfield, Iowa, preschool classroom. In 1993, when Rheta became the director of the Regents' Center for Early Developmental Education at the University of Northern Iowa, she met Christina and immediately recruited her as a graduate assistant and, later, research associate, Freeburg teacher, and Freeburg curriculum coordinator. During visits in Christina's classroom, we discussed children's thinking in various physical-knowledge activities, including Inclines.

When the Regents' Center formed its first Teacher Practitioner Council (TPC) in 1998, incline activities were among those shared with the group. Subsequently, one of the TPC members, Sharon Doolittle, began using inclines in her Prairie City, Iowa, preschool classroom in 1998. While browsing through an old resource (Gilbert 1984), Sharon noticed a photograph and brief description of an incline (ramp) activity using 1-foot lengths of narrow cove molding, sponges as supports, and cars and other objects to try to roll down the slope.

Sharon was inspired to develop this idea, making use of the principles of teaching suggested in *Physical Knowledge in Preschool Education* (i.e., encouraging children's initiative, intervening to foster thinking, etc.). Sharon shared with us the idea of using cove molding as ramps. Christina, who was then teaching in a Head Start classroom with co-teacher Gwen Harmon, expanded this activity by using a variety of lengths of molding up to 4 feet long. We were thrilled to see children's excitement and depth of engagement as they tried out their ideas.

In 2001, the Regents' Center and the College of Education at the University of Northern Iowa built and established the Freeburg School, a laboratory school for children ages 3 to 8. The Freeburg School was located in a low-income neighborhood of Waterloo, Iowa. At the school, 85–92 percent of children qualified for free lunch, and more than 70 percent were African American.

From 2001 to 2007, we were part of a team of teachers; special educators; specialists in early childhood, music, art, science, counseling, developmental psychology, and media; research associates; graduate assistants; administrators; family workers; and clerical workers who developed and implemented a demonstration of constructivist education. Ramps & Pathways activities were part of a constructivist science program for children and professional development for teachers. The science program eventually included the activities Water Dynamics, Air Dynamics, Sound, Spinning, Bubbles, and Cooking, among others.

As children in Freeburg classrooms worked with Ramps & Pathways, we all became convinced that not only were children learning about the physics of motion; we were, too! Children created more and more complex structures that surprised us. Excitement rippled through the school as teachers called everyone to come see what children had figured out. As time went on, we realized the richness of Ramps & Pathways activities and began to share them with educators locally, nationally, and internationally.

As we learned more, we decided to write a book for teachers that would communicate how a constructivist physical science activity such as Ramps & Pathways can help children learn about force and motion at a practical level so later they can better understand these science ideas at a conceptual level. Funds from the U.S. Department of Education supported the first draft of a manuscript as well as implementation of the demonstration program at Freeburg. A revision of the manuscript was supported by a grant from the National Science Foundation (NSF). That same NSF grant also supported professional development work on Ramps & Pathways, allowing us to invite physicist and science educator Lawrence

NSF-funded work on Ramps & Pathways continues at the Regents' Center at the University of Northern Iowa. For more information, visit the College of Education website at www.uni.edu/coe/.

Escalada to join our team and enrich our understanding of the laws of motion. This book presents some of the results of teachers' classroom research on Ramps & Pathways, most of which was conducted at the Freeburg School.

About this book

This is a book about movement of marbles and other objects along sections of track that we call "pathways," including inclined pathways, which we call "ramps."

It adds to the body of work on constructivist early childhood education that has been developed over 40 years. It extends the work on physical-knowledge activities begun in *Physical Knowledge in Preschool Education* (Kamii & DeVries 1978/1993) and continued in *Developing Constructivist Early Childhood Curriculum: Practical Principles and Activities* (DeVries et al. 2002). It reflects the work of children and teachers with Ramps & Pathways activities in constructivist classrooms. Piaget's theory of how children "construct" knowledge and intelligence illuminates these practical accounts. It shows how *teachers can think about children's thinking* in the context of the classroom—a distinguishing characteristic of constructivist teaching.

In chapter 1 we explain what we mean by a "constructivist" approach to teaching. There we discuss how experiences in Ramps & Pathways foster the development of intelligence and knowledge. In chapter 2 we describe constructivist physical science education. In chapter 3 we focus on the "mental relationships" that children have the possibility to make about the physics of motion during Ramps & Pathways activities. How to work with children in these activities is the topic of chapter 4 on principles of teaching.

Teachers who believe in children's play and exploration, but have struggled with how to explain its educational value, will find the theoretical foundation (rationale) in this book especially useful. Some people who observe children working with ramps may think they are "only playing." Children themselves may view what they are doing as play, because it is pleasurable. We, however, see children in these activities as interested, focused, purposeful, intellectually and emotionally engaged, and learning from their errors—all characteristics of productive work recommended by John Dewey (1913/1975) as well as Piaget (1948/1973). In fact, much of what people call play, Piaget called work.

Although we offer practical suggestions for using ramps activities with children, we do not intend to present them as recipes to be followed. Rather, we hope teachers will find ingredients to inspire their own classroom experimentation. Study groups may want to use the book as a focus for discussions about their own experimentation.

Finally, we want to emphasize that children need time and experience to derive the full benefit from ramps activities (as well as from other physical-knowledge activities). Some examples in this book may lead teachers to expect that children's knowledge about ramps develops quickly. On the contrary! The children who make the more complex structures we describe have had years of experience. Be patient. Most children experiment with the same problems of force, motion, and the like for some time before they construct complex knowledge about the phenomena. Expecting too much too soon can interfere with children's processes of testing their many incorrect and correct ideas. On the other hand, if children do not try anything new on their own, the teacher must intervene with questions, suggestions, or challenges to spur their interest and encourage further experimentation.

As you will see in chapter 1, it is only through working to solve problems that interest them that children can construct their understanding of the physical world.

"Give the pupils something to do, not something to learn; and the doing is of such a nature as to demand thinking; learning naturally results."

—John Dewey, *philosopher and education reformer*

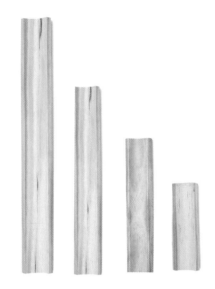

Ramps Materials

This book focuses on one type of Ramps & Pathways material that we find is particularly interesting to children: narrow lengths of cove molding, 1¾ inches wide and cut into lengths of 1, 2, 3, and 4 feet.

Cove molding. Cove molding is a decorative wooden edging used to conceal the seam between ceiling and wall around the perimeter of a room. It can be purchased at builder supply stores. The particular type of cove molding we discuss in this book has a flat back and a single groove down the center. This groove forms a ready-made path that suggests continuation. Other useful pathway materials are sections of plastic rain gutter, like Erica used; transparent flexible tubing of varying diameters and lengths; and cove molding in smaller and larger widths.

A constructivist approach stresses that materials should intrigue children and inspire ideas about what to do with them. This versatile material appeals to children (as well as adults) across a wide range of ages and developmental levels. Children find making ramps and pathways with cove molding fascinating for years because this material lends itself to posing more and more complex structural challenges.

Cove molding can slip and slide easily. Small pieces of rubbery shelf lining or flat foam underneath the ramp sections can help hold them in place.

Adequate space. Working with ramps requires enough space for several children to build at the same time. Space requirements also depend on the overall size of structures children are building. Teachers at Freeburg School noticed that children usually begin experimenting alone, with a single ramp section, which takes up little space. Then they begin building side by side, making long, straight pathways by connecting the single inclined section to several additional sections flat on the floor. Later, when their teacher challenges them, older children build multilevel pathways in confined, taped-off areas (see, e.g., Photograph 22 in chapter 3).

We have worked with teachers who deal with limited space by allowing children to build under and over desks, over shelving, and behind the furniture around the perimeter of the classroom. When possible, arrangements that allow children to work on and enjoy their structures over more than one day are ideal. If materials need to be put away, teachers can take a digital photograph to show children how to recreate a structure later.

Variables. A wide variety of *supports* to hold ramps at a particular angle, different *objects* to travel down a ramp or along a pathway, and different lengths of cove molding give children opportunities to experiment and possibilities to construct mental relationships (knowledge) involving these and the additional "variables" of *slope, connections, targets,* and *pathway designs,* as discussed in chapter 3. Many classrooms already have a selection of blocks that can be combined with cove molding in a structure or ramp. Children often have ideas that would never occur to adults, such as using furniture and classroom objects as supports. Typically, children use whatever is at hand. At Freeburg, children used shelves, tables, chairs, and even drawer pulls as supports.

*   *   *

Our suggestions for materials are not exhaustive. Our purpose here is simply to help teachers get started with ramps activities that can be extended in a myriad of ways. Inventive teachers are always on the lookout for materials that will present children with novel possibilities for deepening their knowledge and understanding. Sometimes children themselves find objects in the classroom to enhance their experimentation. Teachers and children find it exciting to try challenging new materials or new ways of using old materials.

2

Thinking about Children's Thinking
(Or, Why We Take a "Constructivist" Approach)

Constructivist education takes its name from Swiss psychologist Jean Piaget's theory of *constructivism*. From his research he concluded that children actively create—"construct"—knowledge of the physical world from their experiences when they go beyond what they already know. Piaget's conclusion is now accepted in the early childhood field (see, e.g., Bredekamp 1987; Bredekamp & Copple 1997). We frequently hear and read that "children construct knowledge." In this chapter, we want to delve into the meaning of this statement, specifically into *what* knowledge children construct and *how* they construct it during constructivist classroom activities.

A process of construction

"Constructing" knowledge about the physical world means that children are actively creating, testing, and refining their own original, spontaneous ideas about how things work. Recall the opening vignette. Erica's effort to solve her gravel problem is a small example of the constructive process.

Erica knows from observing Sharon that the gravel on her teacher's gutter is moving faster than her own. However, she does not know how to make her gravel move that way. In an active mental effort to figure this out, Erica focuses on the shovels that scoop and dump the gravel.

When she asks her teacher to trade shovels, Erica shows she has already constructed some knowledge about how the world works. She correctly understands that to achieve a *different* result, she has to change something in what she is *currently* doing. Her idea is that she needs to change her shovel; that is, she forms a *hypothesis* that the shovel she uses to dump her gravel affects how fast the gravel moves down the gutter. She tests her hypothesis (which happens to be wrong; shovels have no effect on how fast gravel moves). Unconvinced by the unsatisfactory result, she tests her incorrect hypothesis a second time: "Can I have your shovel?"

hypothesis

An idea or assumption about how something works, before the idea has been tested.

This hypothesis about shovels and movement of the gravel is original to Erica (and perhaps new to the world!). It is not an idea she was taught by her teacher or parents. So how did she come to it? We can only speculate about her reasoning: Because the shovel Erica uses comes in contact with the gravel, she hypothesizes it must cause the gravel's movement down the gutter.

Children's construction of knowledge is a complex, active process in which their knowledge about the world is dynamic; that is, it is constantly changing. At any point a child's understanding will include correct ideas ("It is possible to make gravel move fast down a gutter so that it falls off the end" and "I have to change something to get a different result") as well as incorrect ideas ("What I have to change is my tool for dumping the gravel"). Understanding that children construct knowledge means that teachers try to figure out how children are thinking in the context of classroom activities—a distinguishing characteristic of constructivist teaching.

The evidence that children construct knowledge of the physical world is that they come up with so many ideas never taught to them about physical objects and object phenomena. For example, during Ramps & Pathways activities we often see young children lay a piece of cove molding flat on the floor, place a marble on it, and then gaze at it expectantly, waiting for the marble to move (see Photograph 3).

3 Seth has positioned a section of cove molding so that it is level. His expectation that the marble will move on its own is clear from his facial expression, body language, and the amount of time that he watches and waits for something to happen.

Consider another example of children's spontaneous ideas about the physical world:

> Three-year-old Josh, who does not understand the necessity of slope for movement of a marble, tries to make a marble go up a slope simply by placing it on the molding and releasing it. He makes many different hypotheses to get the marble to roll upward, including turning the ramp section 180 degrees.
>
> On another day, Josh sees a large marble roll off the end of a ramp section that is almost level. When he tries a small marble, however, it remains motionless. Puzzled that it does not move, he tries adding more small marbles behind the first, one at a time, making a long line of marbles in the groove of the ramp section. Dissatisfied when they, too, remain motionless, he places the large marble behind them (hypothesizing that the marble that moved before will make the small marbles move now). He seems surprised when the large marble fails to push the small marbles.

These kinds of behaviors indicate children's own original and often incorrect ideas about the physical world. These incorrect expectations support Piaget's conclusion that young children think in unique ways, compared with how older children and adults think. Young children do not just have *less* knowledge than adults and older children. The difference is that they so often experience the world in such a way that their knowledge is different in *quality* as well as quantity. For example, Erica did not yet know that it is the gutter's incline that affects how gravel moves; she incorrectly concludes on her own that it is the *shovel*!

Revealing misconceptions

In research on children's thinking, Piaget and many other psychologists found that young children typically have many misconceptions about how the physical world works. Sometimes misconceptions result when children cannot observe an object's movement or reaction. For example, Piaget (1971/1974) studied children's ideas about what makes the last in a line of marbles roll away when the first marble is released to hit the second. He noted that whereas children can actually observe the last marble moving, they cannot observe the force of the hit passing from the first marble to the second, from the second to the third, and so on down the line. To know this internal transmission of force occurs, children would have to make a *deduction*, going beyond what they can see, that transmission must be happening. Young children, however, are not yet mentally capable of that logical deduction.

It is impossible to disprove a young child's beliefs about something that is not observable. For example, some young children (ages 3 to 5) believe that their shadow is a permanent object that has gone inside them or run out of the room when it cannot be seen (DeVries 1986; DeVries & Kohlberg 1987/1990). Similarly, because they cannot see evaporation as it happens (as the liquid becomes gas), many young children believe that magic causes water to disappear. Children cannot test these beliefs, cannot try them out and see what happens. Therefore, they cannot modify the beliefs (until later in their development, when they become capable of logical reasoning about things that are not observable).

deduction

A conclusion come to by reasoning, rather than by direct observation.

For this reason, we recommend physical science activities in which young children can make objects move or change in observable ways. When teachers encourage experimentation with objects such as ramps and marbles, children get opportunities to test their ideas, observe the results, and draw conclusions from their observations. For example, in the introduction, when Erica uses her teacher's shovel to dump gravel on her own somewhat inclined gutter, she can clearly observe how the gravel moves (or does not move, in that instance). She is able to compare her expectation ("Changing shovels will make my gravel go faster") with what actually happens.

When children's expectations are not met, teachers can usually observe surprise, puzzlement, or disappointment in their faces or body language or can hear it in their vocalizations. These feelings can spur children to experiment and try to figure out how to succeed. When objects react in unexpected ways (e.g., when Erica's gravel does not skitter noisily or quickly down her gutter), such feedback offers children the basis for further experimentation.

In fact, a constructivist teacher explicitly encourages children to try out what she as an adult knows to be incorrect ideas. Why? So children will experience contradictions between their wrong ideas about objects and the observable results of their experiments. Observable feedback from the objects is what convinces children eventually to discard a misconception and try out other ideas. This is why Erica's teacher does not correct her idea about shovels. Rather, Sharon cooperates with Erica's initiative in testing what Sharon knows to be an incorrect hypothesis. When a teacher respects young children's unique thinking by giving them the chance to test and refine their incorrect ideas for themselves, they are more likely to go on to correct their misconceptions.

Conventional vs. physical knowledge

Many (nonconstructivist) educators assume that when children have misconceptions, the responsible teacher should show or tell them what is correct. From a constructivist perspective, however, that approach is necessary and productive only when the child's misconception involves knowledge that is "conventional." The term *conventional knowledge* refers to information that is arbitrary—that is, the society has simply agreed that something is so (e.g., "We call that a *block*" . . . "New Year's Day is January 1" . . . "Red means *stop*!"). Remember young Matthew in the introduction? His misconception was that the word *hike* always means "to snap a football through the legs"; his parents supplied the conventional knowledge that it can also mean "walking distances outdoors."

Piaget (1964; 1969/1970; 1971/1974) also talked about *physical knowledge*—that is, knowledge of the physical world that can be gained *only* by active experimentation with objects. Thus, simply showing or telling children about the physical world often results in confused thinking or memorization without understanding. One constructivist first grade teacher, Beth Van Meeteren, encountered this when she taught a summer program for children identified as "talented and gifted": Some children had memorized definitions for words such as *inertia* . . . but then built inclines leading to zigzagged pathways and were surprised when marbles flew straight off the path at the first corner (see Photograph 4).

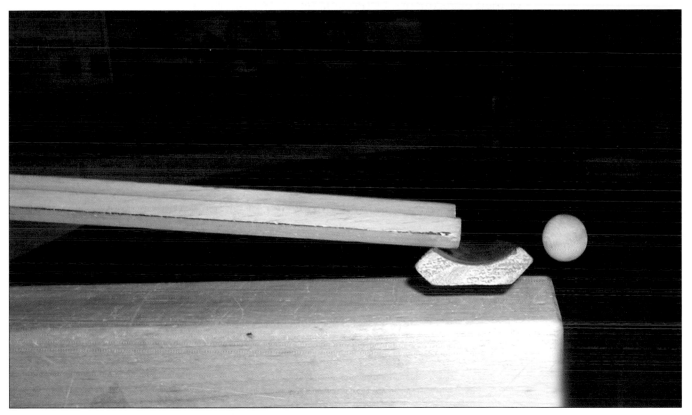

4 When children encounter objects behaving like this wooden ball, they are experiencing Newton's First Law of Motion: that an object at rest stays at rest, and an object in motion stays in motion with the same speed and in the same direction, unless acted upon by an unbalanced force.

Memorization may satisfy requirements for standardized tests. However, it can mislead teachers (and even children themselves) into assuming that children understand the scientific concepts. Piaget, who called such memorized learning "school varnish," worried that it conceals what children honestly think.

Valuing misconceptions

The constructivist teacher values children's thinking and encourages them to test their erroneous ideas. This is a revolutionary and often misunderstood aspect of constructivist education. Valuing misconceptions runs counter to common sense, intuition, and the classic approach of teaching correct facts through showing and telling. Piaget (1948/1973) elaborated his view in a famous statement:

> *The goal of intellectual education is not to know how to repeat or retain ready-made truths (a truth that is parroted is only a half-truth). [The goal] is in learning to master the truth by oneself at the risk of losing a lot of time and of going through all the roundabout ways that are inherent in real activity.* (105–06)

When children's ideas—correct and incorrect—are respected, children feel confident about their ability to think and experiment. In contrast, if children are told when their ideas are wrong:

- They may feel humiliated and make every effort not to reveal anything again about what they think.
- They may not believe the teacher, instead privately holding on to the (incorrect) idea that makes sense to them.
- They may believe the teacher but fail to understand and so conclude they must look to others for correct or acceptable ideas.
- They may come to believe themselves incapable of having good ideas and therefore tend to give up easily.

Children who feel emotionally safe and competent are willing to honestly share their ideas (more on this in chapter 2). This type of environment encourages children to continually create, test, and revise the knowledge they are constructing. According to Piaget, true understanding of the physical world is a "progressive conquest" that can take many years of thinking.

A constructivist teacher's first task is to establish a *cooperative* atmosphere, meaning the teacher respects the ways young children think and the ways they transform their thinking by making new mental relationships.

Constructing knowledge and intelligence

Piaget defined *intelligence* as the sense-making mechanism by which a person organizes his or her experiences. To move beyond the mere fact that children construct knowledge, it is necessary to know that Piaget defined his constructivist theory as a "theory of intelligence or of knowledge" (Piaget & Garcia 1983/1989, 184). By using the word *or* rather than *and*, Piaget was saying that the two aspects (intelligence, knowledge) cannot be separated in a person's experiences. Intelligence cannot operate without knowledge content; knowledge content must be organized by intelligence.

Thus, constructivists view intelligence and knowledge as two sides of a coin—inseparable aspects of the mind. The knowledge content (the *what*) that educators most often focus on is only one side of the coin. The other side is intelligence (the *mental organizing of knowledge*)—that is, the dynamic process of learning. In this view, then, learning is considered from two complementary perspectives: from an intelligence perspective and from a knowledge perspective. As a person constructs one, he or she also constructs the other.

Constructing knowledge

In Piaget's theory, young children construct their knowledge of the physical world by creating, testing, and refining ideas about objects and object phenomena. The product of that process is what Piaget called a *mental relationship*—meaning a mental connection between something and something else that children (and adults) create to organize and thus make sense of their experiences.

For example, a child who rolls marbles across tiled and carpeted floors may create a mental relationship between *texture* of the floor and *distance* a marble travels off the end of a ramp. What the child actually thinks is probably something like, "On smooth tile, the marble rolls a long way; on not-smooth carpet, it rolls only a little bit. The marble rolls farther on a smooth floor." She has learned something about the motion of marbles (knowledge).

Another way to say this is that the creation of a mental relationship in physical science is the linking of variables—where a *variable* is something that can be changed. In the above example, texture and distance are the variables. That is, the child may come to understand that if she changes the surface she makes her marble roll across, it will change how far her marble goes.

Such understanding (e.g., about the motion of marbles) is the *what* side of the coin—knowledge the child constructs in the form of a mental relationship (between texture and distance).

Constructing intelligence

As the child constructs knowledge, she also constructs her own intelligence—the *mental organizing of knowledge* side of the coin. That is, in the act of constructing a mental relationship (e.g., about the motion of marbles), she is organizing knowledge (by classifying, seriating, etc.). Moreover, as the child constructs more and more mental relationships, she becomes more and more intelligent.

This is contrary to the definition of intelligence behind the design of IQ tests, where a person's "intelligence quotient" is assumed to be inherent and unchanging. In Piaget's theory (1975/1985), intelligence is not static. Rather, intelligence is a dynamic process. As a child constructs more and more mental relationships, her intelligence becomes more and more powerful and capable of organizing knowledge content.

Constructivist teachers believe, therefore, that when they value and encourage a child's unique thinking about the physical world and how it works, they are not just fostering the child's construction of specific physical knowledge. Through asking provocative questions and making provocative comments, teachers are also fostering the child's construction of intelligence.

Chapter 3 expands on Piaget's notion of *mental connections/relationships* and *variables* and describes some of the mental relationships children can construct during Ramps & Pathways.

*　　*　　*

Our constructivist goal as teachers, then, is to help children become more intelligent as well as more knowledgeable. Of course, constructivist teachers develop curriculum that meets society's requirements for *what* children must know and be able to do. Constructivist teachers take a leadership role in demonstrating how many of those knowledge requirements can be embedded in activities that still respect *how* children think and learn. Activities with ramps and pathways are excellent for this, as we will describe in the next chapter.

5

Doing Constructivist Physical Science

The main foundation of our constructivist approach to doing physical science is Piaget's research-based theory because his work helps us understand how children acquire knowledge of the physical world. Although Piaget's research did not focus on education per se, his theory does address a question of fundamental concern to all educators: How is new knowledge acquired?

In chapter 1 we described one of Piaget's conclusions from his research—that children construct knowledge. Not only do they construct the knowledge *content*, but they also construct the intelligence that *organizes* knowledge. In this chapter we describe more of Piaget's ideas that influence our approach (constructivist education) to doing physical science in the early childhood classroom.

According to Piaget, children learn by encountering problems they feel compelled to solve; experiencing emotions such as puzzlement, curiosity, surprise, and frustration; and engaging in the intellectual and emotional work of overcoming obstacles to solving those compelling problems. It is through this process that children make the mental connections (*mental relationships*) that are the construction of knowledge or intelligence. The role of the constructivist educator, therefore, is to provide children with an environment that makes this process possible.

mental relationship

A mental connection between ideas, created by the child to make sense out of his or her experience of how things work in the world.

When people ask for a definition of *constructivist education*, we like to say that it has three elements: interest, experimentation, and cooperation (DeVries & Kohlberg 1987/1990). *Interest* drives the constructive process and motivates children to think and acquire new knowledge and understanding. *Experimentation*, informed by observable feedback, leads children to a more complete understanding of physical phenomena. *Cooperation* describes the type of social atmosphere children need for the optimal development of knowledge and intelligence and the development of emotional, social, and moral aspects of personality.

Interest

According to Piaget (1954/1981), interest is the "fuel" of the process by which children figure something out (knowledge) and, at the same time, become more able to figure things out (intelligence). Only if they are interested will children invest the energy and effort necessary to construct new knowledge and understanding. Children will devote prolonged effort when activities are emotionally and intellectually satisfying.

Piaget pointed out that effort is most productive when children's interest is thoroughly engaged. (This is true even for adults.) The constructivist teacher's challenge, then, is to identify which phenomena, ideas, materials, and so on, are most engaging. In our experience of doing physical science, we have found that Ramps & Pathways activities especially intrigue young children (and adults) and arouse in them a need and desire to figure out something.

In other words, Piaget's (1954/1981) view of affective and personality development is integrated with his theory of intellectual development. (By *affective*, he meant something like "emotional," including feelings.) According to Piaget, all mental relationships have an affective component in addition to intelligence and knowledge (cognitive component). One of the affective aspects of a mental relationship is interest (e.g., whether the child *wants* to figure out how to make gravel move more quickly down an incline). The cognitive aspect is what the child understands: "I need a different shovel" (incorrect) or "This shovel doesn't make my gravel move faster" (correct).

For Piaget, affectivity is the energy source on which intelligence depends, like "gasoline which activates the motor of an automobile" (1954/1981, 5). Affectivity can stimulate or hinder the construction of mental relationships. Intensity of interest, in particular, is a regulator of energy put forth. About the range of emotions the constructive process can involve, Piaget (1954/1981) wrote,

> *While working, states of pleasure, disappointment, eagerness, as well as feelings of fatigue, effort, boredom, etc., come into play. At the end of the work, feelings of success or failure may occur; and finally, the [child] may experience aesthetic feelings stemming from the coherence of his solution. (3)*

Thus, for Piaget, affectivity infuses the constructive process and influences whether the child succeeds or fails in solving a problem. As we all know, children (adults as well) who feel confident, are willing to persevere, and invest great effort often succeed. Even negative feelings such as frustration and anger may not dissuade the child from continued effort; rather, they may motivate the child to try harder and focus more closely on a problem. Conversely, feeling inferior or indifferent may prevent a child from wanting to make much effort to figure out a problem, even when she might be capable of doing so.

> Sherronda, a 5-year-old, gives up and cries in frustration when her marble keeps jumping off her ramp structure. Her feelings of inadequacy and failure prevent her from thinking about new possibilities for repairing her ramp, until a teacher helps her regain control and focus. After succeeding with the teacher's help, Sherronda gains confidence, she feels pleasure in her success and new understanding, and she renews her work with enthusiasm.

For a constructivist teacher, these ideas have an enormous influence on planning curriculum—in fact, on planning, implementing, and evaluating every aspect of a classroom day. The teacher will factor in her anticipation of children's interest when deciding about curriculum, including types of activities, materials, and possible interventions. In the course of implementing activities, a teacher evaluates children's levels of interest and emotional investment in the work.

A child's intrinsic interest can be provoked by an external (extrinsic) source such as materials provided by the teacher and teacher interventions that encourage the child to figure out how to do something.

> The teacher in the 3-year-olds classroom notices the children are losing interest in their long straight pathways. She gives each child a small bucket and asks, "Can you figure out how to make your marble roll into the bucket?" Immediately, the children's interest is renewed.

The constructivist teacher watches to see whether these external suggestions become children's intrinsic interests. For example, when a child builds the same ramp structure day after day without changing it in any way, the teacher might ask, "Can you figure out how to make your marble go all the way across the classroom?" or "Can you make a marble go up a ramp?"

The teacher also watches to see whether children find challenge in an activity. If the activity is too easy, children do not make new mental relationships. If it is too difficult, children may be so overwhelmed that they cannot make new mental relationships about the content; they even may, unfortunately, make a relationship between the content and feeling inadequate ("This marble won't stay on the ramp. I don't know what to do. I hate ramps!").

Experimentation

Experimentation with physical objects (i.e., acting on them in various ways) is essential to the mental process of constructing physical knowledge. By definition, experimentation inevitably involves many efforts that do not work out as expected. Piaget (1975/1985) called the mental process that guides experimentation *equilibration*.

In the following section, we describe the process of equilibration and how understanding the process helps us appreciate how children construct new knowledge.

Equilibration

Equilibration is Piaget's (1975/1985) term for the process of mental development. In physical science with young children, the process involves experimenting to figure out how to do something (e.g., how to make gravel slide quickly down a gutter). Another way of saying this is that equilibration is the process of making a new mental relationship (correct or incorrect).

Equilibration includes moments of uncertainty, or *disequilibrium*. One kind of disequilibrium results when what actually happens is not what the child expected. For example, children often place two ramp sections at a right angle and expect a marble to turn the corner. Instead, it continues in a straight line, as seen here.

When a child's expectation is not met, the disequilibrium is both an intellectual and an affective experience. The intellectual part of disequilibrium comes when the child recognizes a *contradiction* to her expectation ("Hey, the marble didn't turn the corner"). The affective part is when she feels puzzled, frustrated, or surprised by this unexpected result. Her disequilibrium may be slight or strong. It is the discomfort of disequilibrium that motivates children to seek solutions ("That's not what I wanted to happen. How can I make it turn the corner?").

Each time the child tries out an idea that turns out to be erroneous, the observable result informs her next effort. She may try many possible solutions, make various errors, and observe how the marble moves with each new idea. We call this process *error-informed experimentation*.

With each equilibration, children change *what* they know (knowledge content), and they become better at *mentally organizing* that content (more intelligent).

Through error-informed experimentation, the child may come to construct a network of mental relationships that reflects her understanding of how marbles move and corners are formed. We say she has attained a temporary *equilibrium*. As she encounters new problems, the equilibrium will be followed by new disequilibria, followed by equilibrium again. In this way, the child moves toward a more complete understanding of the many aspects of building more and more complex ramp structures. Better understandings enable her to anticipate and avoid potential ramp problems, and she eventually becomes able to build a ramp structure where the marble turns corners, drops from one section to another, goes up an incline, and so on.

This is how all learning is acquired—through a continuing process of disequilibrium and equilibrium, then another disequilibrium, and so on.

Sometimes disequilibrium might be so strong that the child abandons a problem. The child might respond to a contradiction to her expectation by not accepting the result and repeating the same action over and over again—Erica did that in the introduction. Such a child does not make new mental relationships until she decides to try something new.

Sometimes an equilibration occurs so quickly that the disequilibrium is hardly noticeable. For example, teachers see this when a child observes his marble shoot straight off the end of the first ramp section, instead of turning a corner onto a second section, and he immediately places a block at the end of that first ramp. That the child realizes he needs the block as a deflecting object shows he has that quickly constructed new mental relationships among the deflecting block, the two ramp sections, and the movement of a marble.

Physical-knowledge activities

As noted in chapter 1, by *physical knowledge*, Piaget was talking about knowledge of the physical world that can be gained only through physical experiences with objects and object phenomena. When the child acts on (does something to) an object and observes its reaction, she finds out what can be done with the object. The source of physical knowledge is objects. By pushing balls and cubes, she learns that balls roll but cubes slide; by dropping various balls, she learns that some balls bounce. Ramps & Pathways activities are in a category of physical-knowledge activities having to do with the *movement* of objects—that is, the physics of mechanics.

To promote children's physical knowledge, the constructivist teacher encourages them to experiment and learn from the objects' reactions. For example, through experimentation, children may learn that a marble regularly rolls

chemistry

A second category of physical-knowledge activities, having to do with *changes* in objects.

downward on an incline. In "physical-knowledge activities" (Kamii & DeVries 1978/1993), a child might, for example, aim balls of different sizes to make a target fall; pour water into cups with holes in their bottoms and sides on a pegboard to make water fountains; cook muffins; or mix flour and oil to make playdough. In such activities, children can engage directly with objects and figure out how the world of objects and object phenomena works.

Constructivist teachers respect children's spontaneous, error-filled and error-informed experimentation as a form of the *scientific method* that real scientists follow. But our reasons for recommending physical-knowledge activities go beyond the value of the scientific method itself. Piaget's research and theory—and our own classroom work—demonstrate that physical-knowledge activities help children to construct knowledge and intelligence.

Good physical-knowledge activities intrigue children to figure out how to make something happen. To provide optimum opportunities for children to experiment and make new mental relationships, what happens must be:

- *producible*: the child must be able to produce "what happens" with his or her own actions;
- *immediate*: "what happens" must occur as soon as the child acts on the object;
- *observable*: the child must be able to see something happen; and
- *variable*: the child must be able to vary his or her actions to produce and observe variations in the object's reactions (Kamii & DeVries 1978/1993).

Activities with ramps and pathways meet all these criteria.

Constructivist teachers focus on helping children figure out how to make things happen even though children do not (cannot) yet understand the scientific principles involved. That is, a teacher doing Ramps & Pathways activities helps children figure out how to make spheres roll upwards, turn corners, go farther, and the like, knowing that they do not understand the principles of mechanics.

According to Piaget, development of knowledge evolves. At first, children are capable of "knowing how" to produce an effect; that is, they can construct

The scientific method

1. Observe a physical phenomenon
2. Ask a question / define a problem
3. Make a hypothesis
4. Experiment to address the problem / test the hypothesis
5. Observe/analyze the result of the experiment
6. Develop a conclusion

Like real scientists, young children working in Ramps & Pathways make and test hypotheses, observe results of error-filled and error-informed experimentation, and conclude whether their hypotheses are correct or incorrect.

Practical vs. Conceptual Knowledge

When teaching young children about motion using Ramps & Pathways, it is important for teachers to understand the difference between knowledge at a practical level and knowledge at a conceptual level—that is, the difference between knowing how and knowing why. Piaget based this distinction on research in which he found a "remarkable time-lag between [a child's] accomplishment of an action [practical knowledge, or "know-how"] and its conceptualization [knowing why]" (1974/1976, 102).

In his studies, Piaget found that full understanding of the concepts involved with the motion of objects does not develop until about age 11 or 12 (but even then, not in all children). Therefore, it is unreasonable to expect young children to be able to understand or explain physics at a conceptual level. However, as young children construct a practical understanding of motion, they are laying the groundwork for later conceptual understanding.

In light of Piaget's work, the physics curriculum at Freeburg School encouraged children's construction of practical knowledge about the movement of objects. Erica experimented with the materials provided by her teacher to eventually construct the practical knowledge that the slope of an incline and movement of objects on an incline are related. However, at age 4, she could not yet understand the scientific concepts of *gravity, friction, inertia, degrees of slope*, and the like. For children to fully understand these scientific terms, they would need to construct a complex network of conceptual mental relationships.

Constructivist teachers therefore focus on helping young children construct practical mental relationships that precede and foreshadow scientific concepts. For example, children have the possibility to construct the practical mental relationship between steepness of the ramp and distance the marble travels: "Marbles roll farther across the room when I raise the top end of the ramp."

Children (and adults) must first *think* at a practical level about a physical phenomenon before they can understand the physics of that phenomenon at a conceptual level. Therefore, at the practical level we focus on what is observable to children, what is producible by them, and what they can vary in their experimentation (Kamii & DeVries 1978/1993).

what Piaget termed *practical* knowledge ("To make this marble roll, I would raise one end of the ramp"). Later they become capable of "knowing why," or *conceptual* knowledge ("This marble rolls downhill due to gravity"). Teachers of young children, therefore, focus on helping them figure out the practical know-how related to the movement of spheres on ramps. (See the box on the opposite page for more.)

Cooperation

The third element of constructivist education is a sociomoral atmosphere of cooperation. By *cooperation*, Piaget (1932/1965; 1954/1981) meant the type of social context necessary for optimal development of intelligence or knowledge and development of emotional, social, and moral aspects of personality.

A sociomoral atmosphere consists of all the interpersonal relationships among the children and between the adults and children of a classroom and a program or school. In a cooperative sociomoral atmosphere, children feel safe, "securely attached" to the teacher (Howes & Ritchie 2002; Watson & Ecken 2003), and free to be mentally active.

A context of mutual respect

Toward that goal, a constructivist teacher's first task is to establish a sociomoral atmosphere of mutual respect (DeVries & Zan 1994; DeVries & Zan 1995). In contrast to interacting with children in a controlling or coercive way, practicing mutual respect means that not only are children expected to respect their teacher, but the teacher reciprocates by respecting each child. The goal is to learn to take the perspective of others and operate in terms of one another's feelings, desires, and ideas. In particular, this means the teacher respects the ways in which young children think and the ways they transform their thinking by making new mental relationships.

A cooperative teacher-child relationship is central to establishing the kind of environment in which the child feels free to experiment, free to make mistakes without feeling inadequate, and free to share his or her thoughts with the teacher

Cooperation vs. Coercion

Piaget distinguished two types of adult-child relationships: *cooperative* and *coercive* (controlling). Advocacy of cooperation and criticism of coercion have been misunderstood by many people as advocating permissiveness—that is, allowing children to do anything they want. We do not advocate permissiveness. For Piaget, cooperation was an essential characteristic of "active education" that respects the ways in which children think and the ways they transform their thinking. It is by fostering children's thinking that a constructivist teacher can help them construct moral values and convictions about how to treat others, as well as truths about the physical world.

Cooperating with children means that the constructivist teacher refrains from *unnecessarily* controlling children. The goal of the constructivist teacher is to *minimize* external control to the extent possible and feasible, and to promote each child's internal control. Teachers help children help themselves. How this works in practice is a subject for extensive reflection on the part of teachers as they consider their interactions with children.

Even though constructivist teachers avoid unnecessary control of children, external adult control is sometimes necessary. In these instances, it is important to empathize with the child, explain why the child must comply, and be firm but not mean. Teachers struggling with the distinction between firm and mean have found it helpful to examine their emotional state, body and facial expression (especially the eyes), and tone of voice. Constructivist teachers are always trying to help children exercise some degree of self-control.

Note: For further discussion of mutual respect see *Constructivist Early Education: Overview and Comparison with Other Programs* (DeVries & Kohlberg 1987/1990) and *Moral Classrooms, Moral Children: Creating a Constructivist Atmosphere in Early Education* (DeVries & Zan 1994).

and peers. A teacher who is controlling or intimidating can stifle children's actions and thinking. A warm acceptance of each child, genuine interest in what the child is trying to do, and a sympathetic attitude are essential.

In physics activities such as Ramps & Pathways, this is important in relation to children's testing of their erroneous ideas, as discussed in chapter 1. If children's ideas—correct and incorrect—have been respected, they feel confident about their ability to think and experiment. A teacher respects a child by observing to understand the child's thinking. For example, in chapter 1 (and here), we see Seth waiting patiently for the motionless marble to move on a level ramp. It seems clear from Seth's actions that he expects the marble to move on the ramp.

What a respectful teacher does depends on what Seth does next. If it appears that he is going to abandon the activity, the teacher will try to encourage thinking about what to change to get the marble to move: "What do you want the marble to do?" or "What could you change to get the marble to move?" Using the word *change* often communicates to children the possibility of trying something they have not tried before. If Seth continues to experiment, the teacher might decide not to intervene at all or might engage emotionally in the effort by staying close and making it clear to him that she is interested. The presence of the teacher in the activity makes a statement that what the child is doing is valuable. Also, she might say something such as, "I see you have another idea" or "Sometimes you have to try lots of different ideas before you get it to work."

A constructivist teacher helps children put aside their usual view of adults as their superiors, the "experts" who already know everything, by relating to children as a companion or guide. Teachers can express respect for children in a variety of ways. They might:

- conduct class meetings to discuss and evaluate how the classroom is and how they want it to be (see also Developmental Studies Center 1996);
- selectively allow children to make decisions about classroom procedures and curriculum;
- encourage children to discuss and make rules they feel are necessary to prevent or solve problems;

- conduct discussions about interpersonal problems they read about in story books and experience in their classroom; and

- engage children in conflict resolution, with the goal of their learning to take account of another's point of view and resolve their own conflicts.

Such activities are described and discussed in *Moral Classrooms, Moral Children* (DeVries & Zan 1994).

The constructivist classroom context

The constructivist classroom context for physical science embodies the characteristics of mutual respect.

The constructivist teacher gives children choice during Activity Time among such activities as pretend/dramatic play, reading books, group games, painting, listening to and acting out stories, playing musical instruments, and physical-knowledge activities such as hitting a target with a pendulum, making fountains with water, making bubbles, making objects move using air, spinning objects, building with blocks, and cooking.

The teacher also especially designs activities to create community and promote social and moral development (DeVries & Zan 1994).

Curriculum areas such as literacy, mathematics, and social studies are important, too, and are often integrated in themes and projects stemming from children's interests, the first element of constructivist education. For example, using photographs or their drawings of their ramp structures, children can dictate or write about what they have done; the stories can be collected into class books to be enjoyed again and again.*

With older children, the constructivist teacher can conduct small-group readings of trade books and set aside time for Writers Workshops, in which children are often inspired to write about their physical science work. Mini-lessons for the group might involve reading and writing about physical science content and its connections with social studies and mathematics.

*   *   *

Many curricula for young children share aspects of our constructivist approach; but differences often appear in implementation. In particular, constructivist teachers plan not only to teach children content (the *what* of science, language, literacy, and the rest) but also to develop children's intelligence and morality.

We address how constructivist teachers can think about promoting children's intelligence through physics activities in chapter 3.

---

*For more on project work, see *Engaging Children's Minds: The Project Approach* (Katz & Chard 2000), *Young Investigators: The Project Approach in the Early Years* (Helm & Katz 2011), and *The Power of Projects: Meeting Contemporary Challenges in Early Childhood Classrooms—Strategies and Solutions* (Helm & Beneke 2003). The work of these three authors has influenced ours.

6

Mental Relationships
Children Can Construct

As we described in chapter 1, the rationale for doing physical-knowledge activities such as Ramps & Pathways is that as children become more knowledgeable about the physical phenomena in the activities, they also become more intelligent. That is, through the equilibration process described in chapter 2, they change *what* they know, and they become better at *mentally organizing* that knowledge content. At its most basic level, each equilibration is the process of creating of a mental relationship—the "stuff" of which knowledge or intelligence is made.

A *mental relationship* is a connection in the mind, created by the child to make sense out of his or her experiences of the world. For example, in Ramps & Pathways activities, one practical mental relationship that children have the possibility to construct is a connection between the ideas of steepness of a ramp's slope and the distance a marble travels off the end of the ramp ("The higher I build this end of my ramp, the farther my marble rolls across the carpet").

In physical-knowledge activities, young children's intelligence allows them to organize such practical knowledge in networks of mental relationships rooted in action on physical objects. Through the continual modification of mental relationships, children develop the ability to think beyond what they can directly observe, make deductions, and move toward the conceptual knowledge of physics seen in older children.

Two aspects of mental relationships

As discussed in chapters 1 and 2, according to Piaget (1952), every mental relationship has two aspects—a knowledge content aspect and an intelligence aspect.

The first aspect is the specific *knowledge content* that children construct from experimenting; for example, with blocks and marbles and cove molding. As they see what happens, try to make something in particular happen, or figure out how something happened, they form mental relationships about the movement of the objects. For example, as children vary a ramp's slope until a marble travels at just the right speed to turn a corner, they are constructing practical knowledge of phenomena related to the physics of motion.

Such practical knowledge forms the foundation needed for later conceptual understanding—that is, why the laws of motion work. For young children, the goal is to construct knowledge of motion at the practical level.

The second aspect of a mental relationship is *intelligence*, which Piaget defined as a general mental action that can organize any specific content. In other words, intelligence is what a person is capable of doing mentally to knowledge content of any kind.

Piaget talked about some general ways of organizing knowledge content, such as classification and seriation. *Classifying* means to make groupings in terms of similar and different characteristics; for example, "My big marbles and little marbles can both roll." In this example, the sizes of marbles are different, but the way they move (rolling) is the same. *Seriation* involves ordering something (e.g., from shortest to tallest, smallest to largest, first to last in a line, beginning to end of a story); it also means knowing, for example, that the third in an order from shortest to tallest is at the same time taller than the second and shorter than the fourth.

That is, any kind of specific content can be classified; any kind of specific content can be seriated. Any knowledge content can be organized by such mental

Newton's Laws of Motion

1. Objects at rest tend to remain at rest, and objects moving at constant speed in a straight line will tend to continue to do so.
2. When a net or unbalanced force is exerted on an object, the object will experience an acceleration.
3. For every action, there is an equal and opposite reaction.

actions. In Ramps & Pathways, children might think about whether *blue* marbles roll farther than *red* ones or whether *heavier* ones roll farther than *lighter* ones (organizing by classifying). Similarly, children might think about making a marble move along increasingly *steeper* slopes and travelling increasingly *greater* distances (organizing by seriating).

Children are not aware of constructing the intelligence that enables them to organize the knowledge content in ramps activities. They are simply conscious of trying to make a pathway on which their marble moves in the way they want. The evidence of children's progressing construction of intelligence is in their actions.

For example, we frequently observe children figuring out how they can make their marbles go farther by building a higher ramp support. Thus, we can observe how children form a seriation relationship as they exclaim each time the marble goes farther on an increasingly steep slope. The intellectual power (intelligence) of a child increases as he or she continues to organize experiences by making more and more mental relationships.

Knowing that learning knowledge content in constructivist activities such as Ramps & Pathways is interrelated with increasing intelligence (as children actively organize the content) gives teachers a strong rationale for teaching to promote children's construction of mental relationships.

The *pathway* is the track, formed by one or more sections of cove molding, on which the marbles and other objects travel. A *ramp* is an inclined (sloped) pathway.

Variables and mental relationships

Children have opportunities to construct many mental relationships during Ramps & Pathways activities as they pursue their own ideas, encounter problems they want to solve, and figure out how to solve them. In the rest of this chapter, we describe some of the mental relationships children might construct about these *variables* in Ramps & Pathways:

- **Slope**—the incline of a pathway
- **Supports**—what the cove molding sits on
- **Objects**—what travels on the pathway

Variables

One of the characteristics of a good physical-knowledge activity is variability. A *variable* is something that can be changed. In Ramps & Pathways, variables include the steepness of the slope; the method of connecting two ramp sections; the size, shape, and weight of the objects that move (or do not move) on the ramps; and so on.

Young children often change several variables at the same time. For example, if a child wants to make his marble go farther, he may move his ramp to a different floor surface in the classroom, add another block to his support, and use a different marble, all at the same time. The result may be that his marble travels farther than it did before he made all the changes. The problem, of course, is that he does not know which of these changes caused the marble to travel farther.

Therefore, in order to observe the effect of one variable, all the other variables need to remain constant (i.e., stay the same).

For teachers, this means they should be aware of the variables children are changing and make suggestions to help children become aware of the cause of their results. For example, the next time a child wants to make his marble go farther, the teacher might say, "I wonder what would happen if we put just one more block under the top of your ramp." After observing the results of that change, the teacher and child can talk about what happened, maybe add another block, and so on. In this way, the teacher helps the child focus on the variables that he would not think of by himself.

- **Connections**—where one section of molding ends and the next begins
- **Targets**—something at the end of a pathway that an object aims to hit
- **Pathway designs**—structures that children create and build with more than one ramp section

For each variable, we offer just a few examples of mental relationships young children might construct with that variable in mind.

Slope

Figuring out problems that involve the variable of *slope* offers children the possibility of constructing mental relationships such as these:

A mental relationship . . .

- Between the steepness of the slope and the movement of an object (Photographs 3, 8)
- Between the steepness of the slope and the distance a marble travels from the end of the ramp
- Between a series of different slopes and a series of speeds of objects moving down a ramp (Photograph 8)
- Among the angle of a downward ramp, the angle of an adjoining upward ramp, and the distance a marble travels up the next slope (Photograph 8)

When young children begin to build ramps and pathways, they soon figure out that a slope is necessary if they want a marble to move without pushing it. Early in their experimenting with ramps, children often place a marble on a section of cove molding in a horizontal position and wait expectantly for the marble to move, as Seth did back in Photograph 3. When the marble does not move on the level ramp, the feeling of surprise—resulting from the *contradiction* between an expectation and what happens—can motivate children (as it did Seth) to continue experimenting. Children usually become aware that they must create a slope; that is, they usually construct a mental relationship between the slope of a ramp and movement of an object on the ramp.

7
Olivia (sitting at the *end* of her pathway) experiments with making a marble go up and over the crest of her pathway, sometimes jumping from one section of cove molding to another. She is making mental relationships among the steepness of a downward slope, the steepness of an upward slope, and the marble's movement up and over the crest.

8

Laura and KaNeisha experiment in an unusual way with changing the downward slope—and thus the speed of the marble—by sliding the lower end of the first ramp up or down the second ramp. Their plan is to make the marble jump the gap between the second and third ramps.

Once children understand that a marble moves without needing to be pushed when released on a slope, some use the knowledge to try to make a marble roll across the floor as far as possible. They experiment with raising and lowering a ramp section (changing its slope) and observing how far the marble travels across the floor. In this way, they are working out the mental relationship between the steepness of the slope (resulting from the height of the support) and the distance traveled by the marble. (It actually is a coordination of two seriations when children consciously think about both the steepness of the slope . . . *high, higher, highest* . . . and the corresponding distance the marble travels . . . *far, farther, farthest.*)

With experience, some children recognize the need to change a slope when they want to change the speed of a marble (the mental relationship between steepness and speed). Constructing this mental relationship calls for children to experiment with a series of ramps that vary in their steepness to observe corresponding variations in speed.

Making a marble jump from one ramp section over a gap to the next is another problem that children find interesting. The problem is that moving too fast down the first ramp, the marble may jump off the pathway; too slow, the marble may not make it across the gap. Experimenting with slowing down or speeding up a marble can enable children to make mental relationships among the parts of the structure that control speed and the movement of the marble.

Supports

Figuring out problems that involve the variable of *supports* offers children the possibility of constructing mental relationships such as these:

A mental relationship . . .

- Between the two ends of a single ramp (Photograph 9)
- Between the type or arrangement of the supports and the stability of the structure (Photograph 10)

At first, young children do not know how to stabilize a ramp so it does not fall. In Photograph 9a, Ellen focuses on the bottom end of her ramp, ignoring that the top end is sliding off the shelf support. The feeling of frustration as the ramp falls to the floor can lead to construction of a mental relationship between one end of the ramp and its other end. (This is an example of what Piaget called *decentering*—moving from focusing attention on only one aspect of something to taking account of another aspect at the same time.)

Children are often confronted by the results of instability in their supports. For example, sometimes children try to use tall, narrow blocks to support ramp sections. When this unstable support falls again and again, children are forced to face the contradiction to their expectation. This can lead to a need to figure out how to build a more stable structure.

As structures get more and more complex, supports that may have stabilized simple structures no longer do so. This motivates children to search for more satisfactory supports. In the course of experimentation with support materials and arrangements, children revise the mental relationships they had earlier constructed into more adequate ones.

Objects

Figuring out problems that involve the variable of *objects* offers children the possibility of constructing mental relationships such as these:

A mental relationship . . .

- Among characteristics of objects—that is, comparison of objects in terms of weight, size, and so on
- Among characteristics of the objects' movements—that is, comparison of how different objects move down the incline (e.g., rolling, sliding)
- Among characteristics of objects (e.g., weight, size) and speed of movement along the incline

We mainly describe Ramps & Pathways activities in which children use marbles. However, we also use a variety of spheres besides marbles, including ball bearings, ping-pong balls, whiffle balls, small rubber and wooden balls, and so on. We also vary the sizes and weights of spheres, particularly the marbles and ball bearings.

a

b

9

At first, Ellen focuses on the bottom end of her ramp while the top slides off the shelf support (a). Eventually she constructs a mental relationship between the two ends of her ramp, and is able to make it stable (b).

10
Seth and Jonah are using a variety of types and arrangements of blocks to stabilize their pathway. They struggle with different types of supports, stable and unstable (classifying).

Connections

Figuring out problems that involve the variable of *connections* offers children the possibility of constructing mental relationships such as these:

A mental relationship . . .

- Between the direction of the overlap between ramp sections and the marble's continuous travel (Photograph 11)

- Between the angle of the connection (straight, angled) and whether or not the marble remains on the pathway (Photograph 17)

- Between the precise angle formed by adjacent ramp sections and the continuous movement of a marble on the pathway

Understanding these mental relationships regarding continuous movement is particularly key to building more complex structures, such as the ones shown at the end of this chapter. When children are just beginning to make ramps and pathways with more than one section of cove molding, they often do not think about the need for continuity between sections (see Photograph 14).

A common problem occurs when children begin to extend their pathways by adding sections of cove molding. Generally, children add a section to a sloping ramp by placing the end of the new, second section *over* the first (see Photograph 11a), thereby stopping the marble's movement.

To make a successful connection, however, children must anticipate that the pathway needs to be clear of obstacles. Children who have this spatial understanding know how to add to their pathway by lifting the end of the first section and placing the new section *under* the first one (see Photograph 11b). In other words, these children have made a mental relationship between the direction of the overlap and the marble's continuous travel.

a

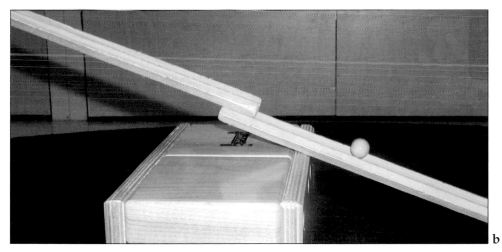

b

11

Depending on how fast the marble is moving when it strikes the misplaced ramp section (a), it may stop or even bounce off the pathway altogether.

A successful connection (b) lets the marble continue its travels.

12
At first, 3-year-old Nathan does not anticipate that the placement of his ramp section (over, rather than under, the next) will stop the marble.

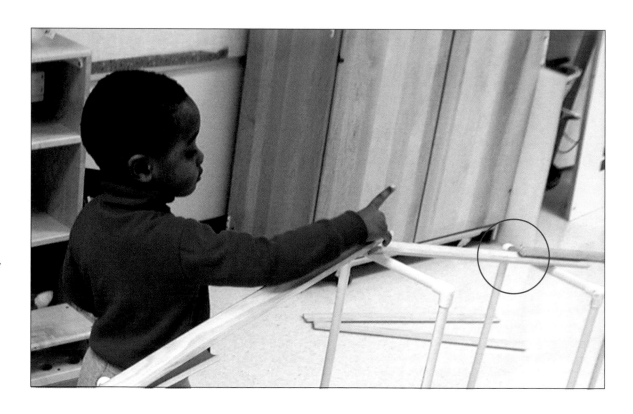

13
Later in the year, however, Nathan watches marbles sail down his pathway past several successful connections.

14
Some children do not anticipate any need for the sections to connect. Jonah is clearly surprised that his car stops between two unconnected sections.

Targets

Figuring out problems that involve the variable of *targets* offers children the possibility of constructing mental relationships such as these:

A mental relationship . . .

- Between the placement of the target and movement of the marble (Photograph 15)
- Between the steepness of the slope and the force with which the marble hits the target (Photograph 16)
- Between the release point of the marble on the incline and the placement of the target (Photographs 15 and 16)

Some children enjoy placing a cup, box, bucket, or other receptacle at the end of the ramp to catch rolling objects at the end of a pathway. We refer to the receptacles as "targets" because in order to catch the object they must be placed in a precise location. Photograph 15 shows the target as a bucket that had to be placed precisely in order to catch the marble.

Pathway designs

Children who have already constructed mental relationships regarding slope, distance, and successful connections frequently invent more and more complicated ramp structures. Figuring out problems that involve the variable of *pathway designs* offers children the possibility of constructing mental relationships such as these:

A mental relationship . . .

- Among parts of a "ricochet" arrangement that allows a marble to turn a corner on a pathway (Photographs 17, 19, 21, and 23)
- Between the end of one ramp and another below when an object is intended to drop from the upper to the lower ramp (Photographs 18, 20, 21, 22, 23, and 24)

- Among the point of a fulcrum, the ramp it supports, the weight of a marble, and the ramp onto which the marble drops (Photograph 20)
- Between the area of floor space for a structure and the design of the pathway (Photographs 18, 19, 22, and 23)

These more complicated structures often present challenging problems. The children who invented the complex ones shown here were first- and second-graders who had worked with ramps for three years.

*   *   *

The mental relationships described in this chapter are only some of the possibilities that children might construct in Ramps & Pathways activities. It is far from an exhaustive list, and its division into groups by variable is artificial. In reality, a complex ramp structure as a whole reflects a network of many inter-coordinated mental relationships that incorporate a variety of variables.

The important message to take from this chapter is that the more mental relationships a child has constructed, the more intellectual power he or she brings to the next situation. That is why Piaget insisted that construction of mental relationships constitutes both intelligence and knowledge at the same time. When the constructivist teacher becomes accustomed to thinking in terms of mental relationships that children might construct, it becomes easier to intervene in children's experimentation in ways that promote such mental constructions—and so help children become more and more intelligent as well as more and more knowledgeable.

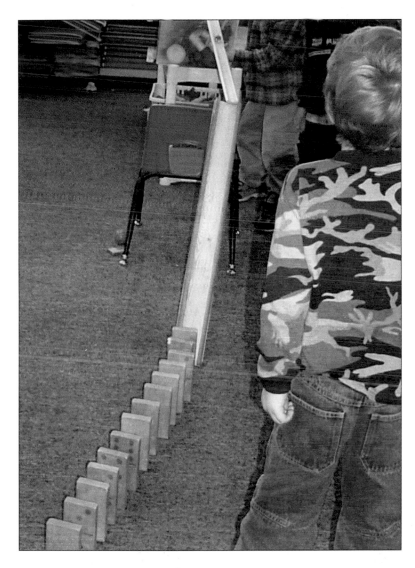

15

Six-year-old Eric watches intently to see if his ping-pong ball (rolling down the ramp) will fly into his carefully placed bucket.

16

William has adjusted the slope of his ramp so the marble will hit the first domino with enough force to set off a chain reaction.

17
Kindergartner Zion figures out how to make a marble turn a corner.

a

b

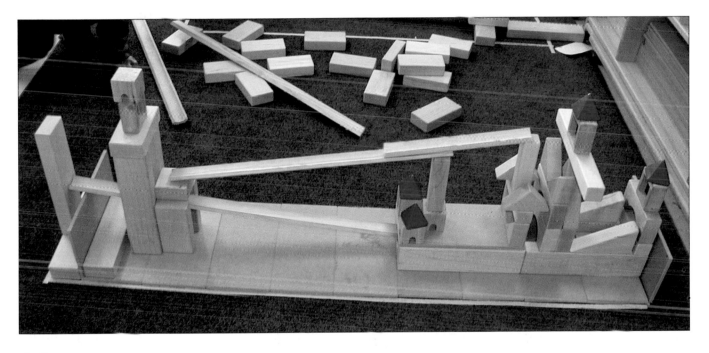

18
A first-grader has arranged ramp sections so that the marble flies between two pillars and falls from one level to the next.

19
First-grader Olivia embeds two right-angle drops in her pathway.

20
**Second-graders built this more complex design with
two working fulcrums and two drops.**

21 Second-grader KeAntre has figured out how far the marble will jump from one section to another. In his design, the marble makes the jump *outside* the tower structure itself. Then, using the shelf and some blocks, he makes a ricochet system that sends the marble back into the structure. This is a work-in-progress, as he has yet to figure out how to connect the next lower level with the end of his pathway.

In an impressive example of error-informed experimentation, KeAntre frequently releases a marble at various points as he builds. He uses the observable results to adjust the placement of the next section of the pathway.

22
Second-graders KaNeisha and KeAntre (not shown) have figured out a response to their teacher's challenge to use many ramp sections in a small area.

23

Second-grader Tana watches a marble traverse her complicated square spiral. A drop inside each corner of the structure forces the marble to make a right-angle turn as it travels down the pathway.

24 This unusual ramp structure (more than 5 feet tall) is built entirely with unit blocks. The close-up shows how the wedges are carefully alternated so the marble falls back and forth all the way to the bottom. Although not seen in the photograph, at the bottom of the ramp structure, the marble rolls out of a tunnel and onto the floor.

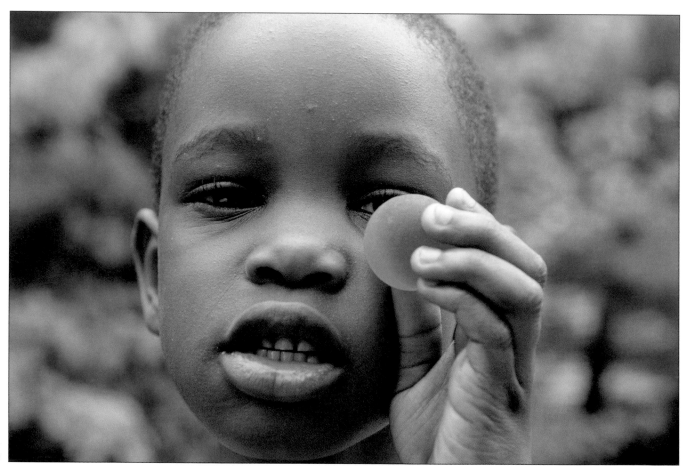

25

4

Ten Principles of Teaching

Working with Children in Ramps & Pathways Activities

Piaget directly inspires our conceptions about how to work with children in general and during Ramps & Pathways activities specifically. He pointed out that "active methods . . . require that every new truth to be learned be rediscovered or at least reconstructed by the [child], and not simply imparted to him" (1948/1973, 15–16). He also emphasized the teacher's role as mentor:

> It is obvious that the teacher as organizer remains indispensable in order to create the situations and construct the initial devices, which present useful problems to the child. . . . What is desired is that the teacher cease being a lecturer, satisfied with transmitting ready-made solutions; his role should rather be that of a mentor stimulating initiative and research. (16)

The following 10 principles of teaching are our interpretations of Piaget's general ideas about how children think and learn best. These constructivist principles were developed with the overarching purpose of fostering children's construction of mental relationships, not only to enhance their knowledge but also to increase their powers of reasoning (i.e., their intelligence).

65

1. Experiment with materials to experience challenges and learning opportunities.

Before introducing ramps to children, teachers need to experiment with the materials themselves in order to understand how interesting the materials can be, become aware of the variables (slope, connections, etc.), and think about what mental relationships children have the possibility to construct.

When teachers experiment first, they can set up challenging problems for themselves and experience emotions similar to children's. For example, teachers can get excited about the activity, wonder about new possibilities, construct hypotheses, and want to test them to observe the results. In addition, teachers will experience disequilibrium upon observing an unexpected result and will go through an equilibration process that leads to new knowledge (new mental relationships).

Once teachers have experimented for themselves, they can then more effectively plan possible interventions (questions, suggestions, or challenges) to help children.

2. Inspire children's interest by introducing intriguing materials such as ramps and pathways.

At group time, the teacher can place a piece of cove molding flat on the floor with a marble resting in the groove and ask, "How can I make this marble move? Do any of you have ideas?" Usually children have many ideas. The teacher can acknowledge children who want to share by asking them to demonstrate what they are thinking about.

Sometimes children's ideas involve blowing on the marble or pushing it with their hands. Then the teacher might say "Can anyone think of another way to make the marble move, without pushing or blowing it?" If children have no new ideas, the teacher might say "I have an idea" and lift one end of the cove molding, sending the marble rolling down. This communicates what an incline can do and how these materials are to be used.

Whenever children begin to generate ideas, the teacher should move children into the activity as soon as possible. "I see lots of you have ideas you want to try. We will have these ramps out during activity time, so you all can try your ideas." If too many children want to work with the ramp materials at the same time, the teacher can suggest they make a sign-up list to eliminate crowding and make sure everyone will have a turn.

The teacher can introduce Ramps & Pathways during Activity Time by building a simple ramp on a table or on the floor in an open area. Children are usually intrigued when their teacher engages in activities (and it is exciting to see a marble fly down a ramp and roll across the table or drop into a container). The teacher can model ways of building ramp structures and wonder aloud for children's benefit, "I wonder if I can catch the marble in a basket" or "I wonder how I could make my marble go farther," then invite them to participate: "Can you help me?"

Once children begin to try their own ideas, the teacher should step back and let the children take over the activity, although still offering support when needed. (We have noticed that sometimes it is hard for adults to turn over this interesting activity to children. Teachers are often so excited about the physics of what they are learning that it is hard for them to refrain from taking over or directing children's experimentation!)

3. Create an environment that inspires children to have ideas and figure out how to do something.

Children's "wonderful ideas"—ideas that are new to a child, especially in a setting where the child is inspired to wonder—are the essence of intellectual development (Duckworth 2006). Duckworth explains that wonderful ideas "need not necessarily look wonderful to the outside world" (14). A key requirement is confidence: "Having confidence in one's ideas does not mean 'I know my ideas are right'; it means 'I am willing to try out my idea'" (5).

Good physical-knowledge activities that meet the criteria discussed in chapter 2 serve as rich contexts for inspiring wonderful ideas. Our experiences with Ramps

Good physical-knowledge activities

Intrigue children to figure out how to make something happen. What happens must be:

• producible

• immediate

• observable

• variable

& Pathways convince us that most children are intrigued by the idea of making a marble roll down an incline and by building more and more complex ramp structures. They are also intrigued by the problems they encounter, and their interest makes them want to invest time and energy in figuring out how to solve those problems.

Piaget's theory, as well as our observations of classrooms, convinces us that children are more likely to have wonderful ideas when they choose an activity than when they are assigned to it. Therefore, we advocate choice (see DeVries & Zan 1994; Piaget 1932/1965). Teachers new to constructivist education often wonder how to give choice without permitting unproductive chaos. Management of many different activities at the same time is a complex process that involves communicating some basic expectations, such as limits for use of materials (e.g., "Be careful with your ramps so you don't hit anyone" or "Don't put marbles in your mouth") and ways to negotiate for desired materials (e.g., "When you are finished with that marble, may I use it?" or "Can I roll my marble on your ramp?" or "Can I build a ramp beside yours?"). Such expectations are the boundaries within which children have choice.

The realities of fostering the sociomoral atmosphere of cooperation described in chapter 2 involve the total interpersonal and physical situation of an active classroom. If Choice/Activity Time deteriorates into chaos, the constructivist teacher stops all activity, calls children together for a class meeting, discusses the unworkable situation, and elicits children's ideas for making the format work. Creating an environment that will inspire children to have wonderful ideas can be achieved only over time as teachers and children learn to live and work respectfully together.

Carrying out wonderful ideas in Ramps & Pathways requires enough physical space for several children to work at the same time. Experimentation with simple ramps and long pathways requires a fairly large open space.

Sometimes it takes more than one day to build a complex ramp structure, and children often want to leave it up overnight. If space cannot be dedicated to leaving the structure in place, a teacher can show respect for a wonderful idea by taking a photograph or making a drawing that satisfies a child's desire for permanence. As children gain respect for one another's work, they may even become able to sit carefully around structures at group time. In the first grade class at Freeburg School, children made a class rule that a ramp could stay up as long as someone was working on it, but once finished it had to come down after two days.

A cooperative sociomoral environment encourages children to be confident about trying their ideas. Fostering a child's development of intellectual autonomy (self-regulation) is the goal. Giving too much indiscriminant praise (i.e., general comments such as "Good job!" or "You're so clever!") keeps the child in a dependent attitude, wanting to please the teacher and focusing on that teacher's evaluation.

It is supportive, however, to appreciate what a child does, especially when he or she wants to share something ("Come look!" or "Wow, I did it!"). Children have a natural desire to share pleasure, and they want to be acknowledged. Specific feedback (e.g., "Look what you can do!" and "You figured out how to make the marble go really far!") promotes the child's persistence, effort, and internal self-satisfaction.

4. Allow children to try out their ideas.

Just having "wonderful ideas" is not enough. Children must have the opportunity to try out these ideas—even ideas that the teacher, with adult knowledge, knows will not work or are incorrect. Even wrong ideas are the result of children's intelligent efforts to figure something out. As discussed in chapter 1, it is through the process of trying out incorrect ideas that children are faced with contradictions and the realization they must change what they are doing and, in turn, revise their thinking (i.e., they must form new *mental relationships*). One of the basic goals of physical-knowledge activities is for children at some point to confront their wrong ideas and be motivated to modify them. For example:

> Before 3-year-old Jaylin understood the mental relationship between the direction of a slope and the direction a marble will travel, he rested one

end of a ramp section on a container and expected the marble to roll
up the slope and into the container. But when he placed the marble on
the ramp, it rolled down—in the direction opposite to his expectation.
His look of surprise informed the teacher that he was experiencing a
contradiction.

In such a situation, it is best for the teacher to share the child's perplexity: "I wonder why it rolled that way? What else can you try?"

Through a recurrent cycle of trying out ideas, observing the results, modifying the ideas, and trying these out, children will eventually reject their incorrect ideas and construct more and more knowledge that adequately expresses how the physical world actually works. The following example illustrates how this process of error-informed experimentation occurs:

In trying to make a marble roll in a semi-circular path (see Photograph
26), KeAntre focuses each time on the point in his marble's travels where
it first rolls off the track. Careful observation informs him that the curve
needs to be more gradual at that point. He moves the ramp section
slightly to decrease the curve and releases the marble again. Again, the
marble rolls off the track. He moves the ramp section slightly to further
decrease the curve. This time the marble rolls smoothly across the
connection and onto the next ramp section.

During his work, each error was a source of new information that led KeAntre to a new hypothesis and a new adjustment, testing the mental relationship he had made between the curve of the structure and the movement of the marble.

Error-informed experimentation is not the same thing as random trial-and-error. Random trial-and-error means making a series of arbitrary changes; error-informed experimentation means making changes based on relevant information from the results of previous experiments. KeAntre continued to use the results of his experimentation to inform the completion of his semi-circular structure.

26 To build this very precise structure, KeAntre went through an extended cycle of hypothesizing, trying out the ideas, observing, and modifying his hypotheses.

5. Observe children's actions to understand/assess their reasoning.

Before asking children questions, the constructivist teacher observes what children are doing and tries to understand/assess how they are thinking. Children's actions can reflect their hypotheses and therefore provide clues to their reasoning. When teachers base a question on their observations, it is more likely to follow the child's train of thought and therefore promote the child's progress.

Even experienced constructivist teachers sometimes forget to observe closely before asking a question. They are confronted with the inappropriateness of their intervention when the child ignores them or abandons the activity. One of us had this experience:

> Christina is interacting with 3-year-old Ty while he builds a horizontal ramp (a level section of cove molding, its ends sitting on two blocks). He places his marble on the molding and pushes it, so it rolls to the end and drops off. Because Christina's agenda is to help Ty learn about slope, she asks, "What can you change so you don't have to push your marble?" (This, by the way, would be a very good question in many circumstances; in this case, however, it is not.) At first, Ty simply ignores Christina. When Ty does not respond, she asks the question again. He ignores her again. After Christina asks for the third time, Ty stands up and walks away from the activity.

As Christina reflected on her ineffective intervention, she remembered that earlier in the day Ty had been making inclined ramps, on which he was letting go of his marble and watching it roll down the slope. Had she not been so focused on her agenda about slope, she might have remembered his earlier actions and made more of an effort to observe him closely now—in other words, to try and figure out what he was thinking about and what he was trying to do.

Had she done that, instead of asking her question, she might have made a comment such as, "I noticed that earlier you were letting go of the marble on the slope, and now you are letting it go on a flat ramp." This comment might have encouraged Ty to compare the results of his two different actions. Intervening in such a way would have been based on her observing Ty's current actions and trying to figure out what he was thinking. The comment might have stimulated him to make a mental connection about something he was already doing and interested in. But Christina's question, "What can you change so you don't have to push your marble?" was based on her own agenda. Not only did it fail to get the result she wanted, it also shut down Ty's thinking completely—he left the activity.

The teacher will find it especially useful to watch for signs of children's feelings of contradiction when the result of their actions is not what they expected. For example, when children overlap pieces of cove molding, they expect the marble to roll across the connection. If a child seems surprised when her marble stops or rolls off the ramp due to an improper overlap (see Photograph 11, and here), the teacher knows that the child is experiencing a contradiction between her expectation and the observed result. The contradiction confronts the child with a problem. If the child is highly interested in the activity, a desire to solve this problem motivates her to make adjustments to the two ramp sections to reflect her modified mental relationships.

Observation alone is sometimes not enough to know for certain how a child is thinking. Constructivist teachers sometimes intervene with assessment in mind. Questions a teacher might ask to find out more about what the child knows include:

"What are you trying to make the marble do?"

"Show me with your finger how the marble will go."

"What would you have to do to make the marble go all the way to the wall?"

"Is there anything you can change to make the marble . . . ?"

After understanding what and how a child thinks, a teacher can intervene more effectively.

Ramp Safety

Introducing Ramps & Pathways to children should include discussion of safe ways to use the materials. In our experience, focusing children from the beginning on using the cove molding only as ramps or pathways usually circumvents their use in dangerous ways.

Typically, children simply become so interested in building ramps that they do not want to use the cove molding in other ways. Once, when a 3-year-old pretended a ramp section was a gun, his teacher just reminded him, "Guns can hurt people, so we don't have them at school." When Calvin, carrying around a long section under his arm, was in danger of accidentally hitting someone, we reminded him to "watch where both ends are going." Sometimes teachers suggest that children hold the ramp sections vertically in front of themselves anytime they are carrying them from place to place. (Even just carrying ramps can be an opportunity for a child to *decenter* and think about both ends of the ramp at the same time, as Ellen did in Photograph 9.)

When children want to build above their heads or engage in other potentially unsafe behaviors, teachers can call children together to discuss safety precautions. The teacher can say, "I am worried that someone might get hurt when you are doing that. How can we do _____ safely?" During one such discussion, children suggested that they use a small step stool and the teacher agreed to stand close to them.

Small marbles and other small objects can be dangerous to use with young children. We caution teachers of children who still mouth objects to use only large marbles and other objects that will not go down a choke tube.

6. Intervene with questions and comments to encourage children's thinking (constructing mental relationships).

Children can pursue Ramps & Pathways activities on their own, especially once the teacher has inspired and intrigued them (Principle 2), they see possibilities, and they have ideas they want to try. At times, however, a teacher's intervention can make the difference between a child abandoning the activity or continuing to experiment.

When a child does not know what to do or is too frustrated because he cannot figure out how to solve a problem, a teacher intervention in the form of a question, comment, or suggestion can encourage the child to keep working on the problem. Frequently, young children ignore questions that require a verbal response. They are more likely to respond to questions that can be answered with actions. For example, when asked "What else can you try?" a child can answer by changing his ramp structure.

Piaget's comments on how to teach were few, but he did see a definite place for teacher intervention to promote children's reasoning:

> It is important that [you] present children with materials and situations that allow them to move forward. It is not a matter of just allowing children to do anything. It is a matter of presenting to the children situations, which offer new problems, problems that follow on from one another. You need a mixture of direction and freedom. (Evans 1973, 53)

This advice guides constructivist teachers as they intervene in children's activities. The constructivist teacher intervenes to focus children's thinking on what they have not thought about before. Below we describe five ways teachers can intervene during Ramps & Pathways. (At the same time, we caution that too many interventions can turn off children's interest and cause them to abandon an activity.)

Ask for predictions

After children have experience with Ramps & Pathways, the constructivist teacher asks for their predictions (i.e., ideas or hypotheses about what will happen) to encourage them to reach deeply into their knowledge and use it in a new way. Deep knowledge requires a background of experience with materials that provides some basis for a prediction. Constructivist teachers have learned that it is useless to ask children to make predictions at their first exposure to a physical phenomenon. Without experience with the phenomenon, children have no basis for a prediction about it, and having no ideas can make a child feel inadequate or pressured to say anything, even something nonsensical. As discussed in chapter 1, feeling inadequate undermines children's confidence in their ability to think and experiment.

Once they have had experience, however, the constructivist teacher can ask variations of "What do you think will happen if you . . . ?"

How children act on objects offers clues to their expectations or predictions. For example:

> Four-year-old Carl has worked with ramps and pathways for several weeks when he builds a fancy, zigzagging pathway on the floor at the end of his incline (see Photograph 27). Cheerfully, he calls to his teacher (Christina), "Look what I made!"
>
> Looking at his structure, Christina is surprised that Carl expects the marble to turn even the first corner successfully. From his previous work, she had believed that he had already constructed a correct mental relationship between the slope of an incline and the movement of a marble in a straight line. Christina realizes that Carl is so enchanted with his fancy pathway that he did not, at least in the moment of constructing it, think about what he knew before—that a marble continues its current direction of movement, unless stopped or deflected.
>
> Christina could have suggested that he simply send a marble down the incline, and he would have seen for himself that his idea, though beautiful, wouldn't work. In this situation, however, Christina makes the effort to help Carl anticipate a contradiction to his expectation. Before he releases the marble, Christina asks, "Can you show me with your finger where your marble will go?" Carl traces the pathway using his finger to represent the marble. As he nears the first corner, he stops. Suddenly, he realizes the marble would not be able to turn the corner.
>
> He immediately rearranges the entire pathway, aligning all the sections in a straight line to run straight across the room, all the way to

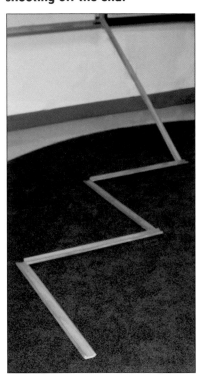

27
Carl's inspiration was the image of his marble whipping through his pathway's corners and shooting off the end!

the wall. As he still has sections of cove molding left over, he continues the pathway by making a right angle at the wall and extending it even farther!

This example illustrates that children may repeat the same error many times in the process of constructing a mental relationship, perhaps with each new problem they encounter. New problems sometimes force children to reconstruct the same relationship over and over again until the knowledge becomes solid. When Carl realized that his zigzagging pathway would not work, he straightened it. However, when his straight pathway ran out of room, he made another corner!

Thus, it is clear that Carl has not yet convinced himself that a marble continues in its same direction only until interfered with. Once children's knowledge is solid, they can anticipate what will happen and prevent problems.

Suggest new possibilities for experimentation

Children often challenge *themselves* to make something specific happen. But even when they have ideas, teachers can make suggestions, too. For example:

> Four-year-old Amy is repeatedly dropping a marble down a ramp. Her teacher thinks this activity has declined into thoughtlessness. He asks, "Do you think you can make the marble roll all the way to the wall?"

In this case, the teacher hopes the child will experiment with the height of the support and think about the relationship between the steepness of the ramp and the distance a marble travels.

A successful intervention can revive children's interest in a problem so that they go on to think of more new ideas on their own. The constructivist teacher's goal is not for the child to follow the suggestion out of compliance or just to please the teacher. The goal is for children to invest their best energies in an activity. As described in chapter 2, this occurs only when children pursue experimentation out of personal interest and a sense of purpose.

Suggesting new possibilities can also take the form of providing additional materials to enrich what children are already doing.

> In a Head Start classroom, Christina asks three children if they would like to see how far their small cars can roll off their ramps. She tapes a strip of adding machine paper to the floor so they can mark where each car stops. Because the children are not thinking experimentally and they do not wonder about changing the steepness of the slope, Christina asks, "What can you do to make the car go farther?" (a question that suggests producing a particular effect).
>
> When it appears that the children still have no ideas, Christina again intervenes. She brings over some more blocks from the block shelf and suggests they might try making the support higher. This idea sparks intense engagement and experimentation to see the effects of different numbers of blocks in the support on the distances the cars travel.

Such specific suggestions should be made rarely, only when children have no ideas of their own and need a catalyst.

Offering possible solutions is also a legitimate intervention when a child is very frustrated. The teacher might give hints—including some that are incorrect—to stimulate a renewed interest and preserve the child's autonomy (self-regulation) in thinking about possibilities. Generally, however, when a child is frustrated, it is enough for the teacher to express sympathy with his efforts and understanding of what he is trying to do.

Here's another example, showing how children can take up a teacher's suggestion and make a new generalized mental relationship that goes beyond what the teacher had in mind:

> After several years of experimentation in Ramps & Pathways using large areas, most children in Beth Van Meeteren's first grade class had constructed a network of complex mental relationships about motion. Beth wanted to inspire her children's purposes with new, exciting, and more complex challenges. So she taped narrow rectangles on the floor,

---

Help in understanding the laws of motion

• NSTA Web Seminar, "Force and Motion: Stop Faking It!" http://learningcenter.nsta.org/

• *Force & Motion: Stop Faking It! Finally Understanding Science So You Can Teach It*, by W.C. Robertson (National Science Teachers Association, 2002).

• Computational Science Education Reference Desk (CSERD), "Bounce" activity www.shodor.org/

• The Physics Classroom www.physicsclassroom.com/Class/newtlaws/

—Peggy Ashbrook

making each about 1 foot wide and 4½ feet long, which was slightly longer than the longest sections of cove molding. Then she gave children two 4-foot-long sections, saying, "I have a challenge for you. Can you figure out how to use both of these to make a ramp inside the taped area?"

After children had worked for several months making more complex structures within various-sized taped spaces, Olivia, a first-grader, reflected on her experiences: "The smaller the space, the harder it is and the more time it takes to build a ramp. The bigger the space, the easier to make and the less time it takes."

Help children become more conscious of what they do

As children pursue their ideas, they often do not notice something that has happened as a result of an action. One way the teacher can focus a child's attention is by stating the teacher's need to better understand a problem (e.g., by saying, "I didn't see where the marble fell off. Could you try that again so we can watch carefully?"). Another way to make children more conscious of what they do is to ask, "How did you do that?" or "Can you show Michael how you did that?"

Children also are not always conscious of what they do, so sometimes it is useful for the teacher to describe aloud what they are doing. For example:

> Five-year-old Lucio does not seem to be paying attention to the fact that he is releasing a marble from different locations on the ramp each time, sometimes at the top, sometimes in the middle. His teacher points this out to him, saying, "I see you put the marble on the top of the ramp last time and this time in the middle, right here." If Lucio is attentive, the teacher might follow up with a question to suggest that he make a comparison: "Does it work better at the top or the middle? . . . Does something different happen?"

Thinking about such comparisons can lead children to a coordination of two or more mental relationships—here, between release at the top and distance traveled, and release at the middle and distance traveled.

Provide counterexamples when children's conclusions contain misconceptions

Sometimes children make incorrect conclusions (i.e., form incorrect mental relationships between variables) on the basis of insufficient evidence. For example:

> A first-grader in Beth Van Meeteren's classroom concludes that marbles always roll *down* an incline. Beth says to the child, "I once saw a child make a marble go *up* a ramp. How do you suppose that could happen?"

Such a countersuggestion is likely to intrigue the child and motivate new experimentation and modification of ideas. Piaget (1973) advised:

> *Teachers should select materials that make the child conscious of a problem and look for the solution himself. And if he generalizes too broadly, then provide additional materials where counter examples will guide him to see where he must refine his solution. It is the materials he should learn from. (23)*

incline

A sloped surface—
In Ramps &
Pathways, a
pathway is the
term for a section
of cove molding.
If the pathway is
inclined (sloped), it
is called a *ramp*.

Encourage children to wonder about physical causes

Most young children are not capable of explaining *why* something happens. In their cognitive development, children must first conquer the know-how of practical knowledge before they are able to consider the why of conceptual knowledge. Asking a young child why questions can imply that the teacher expects a particular answer; it can even make a child feel pressured enough to leave the activity.

Generally, the best approach is for the teacher to comment; for example, "I wonder why the marble on that ramp goes farther than the marble on this ramp?" This open-ended comment leaves the child free to not respond, yet it can motivate her to wonder and think about the reason. If the child does know why, she will likely respond. Piaget (1973) had some advice on this issue:

> *I'd rather ask questions that lead to a practical task and then, once the child has succeeded in this, go on to the question of how it happened. (24)*

Assessment

Young children's learning often is assessed using checklists that focus on behaviors that can be easily counted: how many alphabet letters the child knows, what numerals he can recognize, how high he can count, and so on. Such checklists can provide some important information to the teacher; but they assess children's specific knowledge only.

Children's mental relationships also can be assessed by observing behaviors. Moreover, these assessments provide information on both knowledge and intelligence.

Understanding mental relationships that children have the possibility to construct can help a teacher assess knowledge/intelligence in a new way. That is, if the teacher has ideas about which mental relationships a child has the possibility to construct in a certain activity, she can watch for behaviors during the activity that indicate whether or not the child has constructed a particular one.

For example, say a child positions a ramp section on a level surface, places a marble on it, and waits expectantly for the marble to move. The teacher can infer the child has not yet constructed a mental relationship between creating a slope and the movement of a marble. Say the same child, after several weeks of ramps experience, now always creates a slope at the beginning of a pathway. To check the child's understanding, the teacher could place a marble on a level section of his pathway and ask, "Why don't you start your marble here?" If the child answers something like, "Because it can't roll down," she can be fairly certain the child has now constructed a mental relationship between slope and movement of a marble.

Documenting behaviors that indicate a child's construction or lack of construction of mental relationships is a new and potentially informative method of assessment in any area of development.

7. Do not pursue if a child does not respond to an intervention.

Whenever a teacher intervenes, children need to have time to reflect on their actions and think about the suggested possibilities. Sometimes an intervention inspires children's thinking, and sometimes it does not. In a classroom with a cooperative sociomoral atmosphere that fosters autonomous thinking, children are free to ignore or reject the teacher's offered intervention if they are not interested. If children ignore the comments or suggestions, the teacher just lets the children continue pursuing their own ideas.

Sometimes teachers and children have different agendas. Because children will spend the most amount of mental energy figuring out problems they have set for themselves, the constructivist teacher allows and encourages children to pursue their own problems. When the teacher realizes that a child is not interested in what the teacher has in mind, he must evaluate his idea. If the teacher decides it is important for children to think about, he introduces the idea at another time.

For example, if the teacher wants children to know that marbles will go up a slope as well as down, he might start discussion at a class meeting by asking the question, "Can a marble go up a slope without pushing it?" Children usually disagree about this, and a discussion may motivate many children to take up the problem.

8. Support children's work with representations and discussions of ramps and pathways.

In addition to making something happen that is *producible*, *immediate*, *observable*, and *variable*, an important aspect of a good physical-knowledge activity is children's discussion and representation of the knowledge they construct. In the course of discussing and representing, children have the opportunity to reflect, enrich their knowledge, and share their ideas with others.

Photography is an excellent tool for capturing and saving an image of children's structures. Teachers and children can take photographs with a digital camera to be displayed in the classroom, made into a scrapbook, used by children to write their own books, shown during group times or class meetings to stimulate discussions, or used as documentation of children's work. Even children as young as 4 years old can learn proper and careful use of a digital camera and can take their own photographs of structures.

Until children are able to write their own captions, their teacher takes their dictation ("Look at what you are doing in this picture. What do you want to say about it? I will write what you say"). Teachers share the pen with children as soon as possible. In this way, children have the opportunity to make the mental relationship between their own spoken words and written text. Once children become interested in the writing process, they can begin writing their own captions with the teacher's help. Photographs of their Ramps & Pathways work can provide interesting content for journals. Freeburg teacher Sherri Peterson made a class book of photographs that her 3-year-olds consulted when they needed an inspiration as they built new ramp structures.

Another way to support children's discussions of their work with ramps is through creating drawings of completed ramp structures. For example, following the "teacher as scribe" approach described by Jones and Reynolds (1992), the teachers (or volunteers or children) can sketch a drawing of children's ramp structures during Activity Time. These drawings do not require a high level of artistic ability; a stick figure of the child and straight lines for the ramps and pathways are sufficient. When children see a teacher drawing their ramps, they sometimes begin to draw their own representations. These drawings can be used in the same ways as photographs.

Displays patterned after the Time 1 (beginning drawing) and Time 2 (later drawing) documentation panels made by teachers or children in classrooms using the Reggio Emilia approach (Edwards, Gandini, & Forman 1998) provide a strong record of children's progress. For example, in *Developing Constructivist Early Childhood Curriculum* (DeVries et al. 2002), Rebecca Edmiaston discusses how *webbing*—the visual mapping of children's important ideas and mental relationships—can be an effective tool for promoting dialogue about what children know. Time 1– and Time 2–style webbings can be used to document children's progress. She also offers another example: making wordless picture books using sequenced photographs of ramp constructions (Edmiaston 2002). Children who cannot actually read can use the photographs and drawings as prompts to tell about their ramp structures. Multiple copies of the books are made—for the classroom library, as well as for book authors to take home to share with their families.

Another approach is for teachers or children to write lists of children's thoughts or questions about ramps. Using webbing or lists, children can share ideas about ramps, discuss disagreements, and identify problems they would like to explore. The drawings or photographs also can jumpstart discussions of what children have figured out about ramps. Lively conversations frequently erupt when children present different viewpoints. Many times during these discussions, a child or the teacher poses new challenges to be addressed in the ramp center. Solutions to these challenges can be revisited at later group times.

These are only some of the possible ways in which to encourage children to discuss and represent their ramps work. Children and teachers in constructivist classrooms find daily opportunities to discuss and represent children's wonderful ideas.

9. Integrate all curriculum areas into Ramps & Pathways activities.

Science activities such as Ramps & Pathways are rich with opportunities for teaching and encouraging mathematics, language, literacy, social studies, and art.

Mathematics

Ramps & Pathways materials naturally lend themselves to children's thinking about the quantitative mental relationships involved in number, measurement, geometry, and time.

Piaget (1941/1952; Piaget & Inhelder 1948/1956) showed that children make general *qualitative* mental relationships before they elaborate these into specific *quantitative* mental relationships. Here are some examples:

- Some general qualitative mental relationships about number (e.g., "You have more marbles than I do") are precursors to specific quantitative, numerical mental relationships (e.g., "You have four more marbles than I do").

- Qualitative spatial mental relationships, such as *higher* and *lower* ramp supports, are precursors to specific measurement of "how much" higher and lower.

- Qualitative spatial mental relationships, such as *next to* (e.g., "I'll put this ramp piece next to this one") and *enclosing* (illustrated by the enclosed space of the square spiral in Photograph 23, and here), are geometric notions of connecting lines to form angles and enclosed shapes.

- Qualitative temporal mental relationships, such as *order* ("First, the marble will go here, then it will go there, and then it will fall in the basket"), are precursors to specific measurement of events happening in time ("Your marble hit the wall two seconds before my marble").

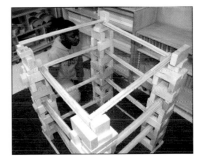

Therefore, children doing Ramps & Pathways activities have possibilities to engage in the kind of qualitative mathematical thinking that leads to quantitative arithmetic, measurement, and geometry.

Language

Language opportunities arise naturally as children talk about their ramps and pathways. Sometimes children have ideas for which they do not yet have words. For example:

> As 3-year-old Darnell uses a big bakery box at the end of his ramp to catch the marble, he makes the prediction, "This big one go out." He means that he expects the large marble to pop out of the box, unlike the smaller marble he used earlier that remained in the box. His teacher, Sherri Peterson, uses this teachable moment to repeat his idea using expanded vocabulary and sentence structure: "You think that the large marble will *bounce* out of the box?"

Teachers will find it is helpful to have vocabulary related to science and mathematics already in mind for such teachable moments when they arise (e.g., *incline, slope, steep, ricochet, stabilize, sphere*), as well as positional prepositions (e.g., *up, down, above, below, around, beside*) and comparison adjectives and adverbs (e.g., *longer, shorter, higher, lower, slower, faster*).

Language opportunities also arise as children express the range of emotions they may feel when their ramps and pathways do or do not work as they expect. This is a chance for teachers to introduce new words such as *happy, sad, frustrated, satisfied, disappointed, angry, puzzled, pleased,* and so on, that people use to describe feelings. In this way, children come to expand their vocabularies as they recognize and label their emotions, important aspects of emotional regulation.

When adults use these words, children often begin to use them, too. However, even children who use these words appropriately may still be in the process of constructing their meanings.

Literacy

As noted in the section on Principle 8 (representations and discussions), teachers can foster children's literacy development by using teacher-assisted writing, making lists of what children know about ramps and pathways, encouraging developmental writing (invented spelling), and adding words to drawings and photographs. These activities contribute to children's beginning learning of reading and writing.

Asking children what they want to say about a single photograph eventually leads to making entire books and, later, to writing personal narratives about building ramps and pathways. Teacher-modeled or teacher-assisted writing supports children's wonderful ideas. For example, a group of three children in a preschool classroom composed the following narrative.

> We made a steep ramp.
> The marble went down fast.
> It fell in the can.

At Freeburg School, teacher Gwen Harmon routinely suggested that the 4-year-olds in her classroom write or draw about their Ramps & Pathways experiences in their journals. As a group, Beth Van Meeteren's first and second grade class filled in a Ramps & Pathways experience chart as a context for integrating science and literacy. She wrote on a whiteboard as children explained what they had figured out, slipping in mini-lessons about letter sounds, blends, word families, punctuation, capitalization, and so on. Children's interest in their Ramps & Pathway activities often carries over into Writers Workshops where they want to record their thoughts about their work.

Social studies

Ramps & Pathways activities provide occasions to think about how real-world ramps help people do work—an aspect of social studies as well as physics. For example, the presence of a child who uses a wheelchair, walker, or crutches helps all children become more aware of the advantage of ramps for moving from one level to another.

Children also can be encouraged to notice other kinds of ramps in their communities, including ramps at crosswalk intersections and driveways, highway ramps, and parking ramps. A dump truck raises its bed to create a ramp, and a moving van lowers its back panel to become a ramp.

In Terry Anderson's first grade classroom in Kirkwood, Missouri, a project on simple machines included the opportunity for children to take turns pushing each other in a wheelchair on a ramp just outside their classroom. That the ramp was adjacent to a set of steps helped them recognize its practical social value as well as physical function. This project went further to integrate literacy into social studies when children wrote letters (which started as sloppy copies and were edited by teachers and children to create final copies) that were sent to managers of public buildings, asking whether they provided handicapped-accessible ramp entrances.

Art

Annette Swann, the art specialist at Freeburg School, noted that the structures children build in Ramps & Pathways share common ground with and are forms of sculpture and architecture. She pointed out that like ramps, sculpture and other art forms involve physical knowledge (children acting on various materials, finding out what happens, and trying to produce particular effects) and representation. They also involve classification (see Photograph 29), geometry (see Photograph 28), and perspective taking, as well as expression of thoughts and feelings. Sculpture and architecture involve both physical knowledge (i.e., knowledge of properties of wood, metal, concrete, etc.) and knowledge of force and resistance, balance, and stability.

At first, children experience cove molding in terms of the physical-knowledge challenges of building successful ramps and pathways. Then, in the course of this work, children learn that cove molding has not just physical but aesthetic properties: *smooth, inflexible, grooved, squared-off at the ends*. After much experience with physical-knowledge problems, first- and second-graders at Freeburg extended their purposes to an entire system of mental relationships in an aesthetic whole that takes on sculptural and architectural meaning (see Photographs 21, 22, 23, and 24 of towers and circular and square spirals). Children engaged in solving physical-knowledge problems often appreciated aesthetic aspects of their beautiful structures and expressed pride, satisfaction, and joy in their creations.

When children build three-dimensional structures, they must reason about space, straight and curved lines, angles, and patterns—all aspects of geometry. In some structures, patterns are repeated and provide unity. Taken as a whole, these geometric characteristics can be thought of as sculpture or architecture.

Just as sculptors and architects consider their designs from various points of view, children, too, look at their ramps and pathways from different spatial perspectives: *top* and *bottom, front* and *back, sides*, and, when possible, *inside* and *outside*. When two or more children work together to build a structure, they must also consider one another's points of view and coordinate ideas.

28 KeAntre's conception was of a rounded structure with a continuous path. He had to construct mental relationships among the straight lines of the cove molding, the angles permitting a marble to move in a semi-circular path, and the angles of the gradually decreasing overall slope.

29 In moving toward sculptural and architectural meanings, children think about various classification relationships, including mental relationships among parts and wholes of pathway designs. KeAntre began with tunnels at the end of the pathway. He then had to think about how to connect each part to form the whole continuous pathway through the towers (see also Photograph 22).

10. Encourage social interaction.

As noted in chapter 2, a characteristic element of constructivist education is cooperative interactions. By that, we mean children's interactions with their teacher as well as their interactions with other children. Cooperation promotes all aspects of development. Piaget stated that "social life is a necessary condition for the development of logic" (1928/1995, 210). Cooperation is of value not only because social and moral development are important but also because cooperative relationships are necessary for optimal intellectual development.

Although physical-knowledge activities such as Ramps & Pathways can be pursued individually, the activities often engage more than one child in trying to figure something out. Children often get ideas to try from others, and excitement and interest are contagious. The teacher also can encourage children to notice what others are doing, which often inspires efforts to imitate and compare results.

Three-year-olds typically work with ramps parallel to one another—nearby, but not collaborating. As children get older, they begin to share their interests as they build. Cooperation often begins when one child asks, "Can I roll my marble on your ramp?" Interested observers often become participants when they see a problem and suggest changes. Eventually, most children want to collaborate in planning and building structures because they find it stimulating and pleasurable to exchange ideas with others. However, children of all ages also enjoy working independently to try out their own ideas.

The pleasure of working together is an impetus to developing interpersonal understanding and friendships. These in turn motivate children both to modify behaviors that interfere with the relationships (e.g., grabbing, hoarding, rejecting) and to learn behaviors that promote the relationships (e.g., sharing, listening, including). When a teacher works together with children, it encourages them to work with one another.

Of course, conflicts sometimes interrupt Ramps & Pathways activities. But children's desire to get back to their experimentation motivates them to find solutions to their conflicts. If they cannot resolve a conflict themselves, they may

The three characteristic elements of constructivist education:

• Interest

• Experimentation

• Cooperation

be especially receptive to the teacher's mediation efforts. Ramps & Pathways activities are good contexts for learning to negotiate and to share experiences. (See DeVries & Zan 1994 for more on how to work with children's conflicts.) Through a process of interpersonal experimentation—akin to experimentation with physical objects—children who are impulsive, for example, can move toward emotional and intellectual self-regulation. As the child interacts with peers, she observes others' reactions to her own actions. If she doesn't get the reaction she wants or expects (*disequilibrium*), she may be motivated to try a different behavior in hopes of getting a different result.

In general, when a child's behavior provokes a negative reaction from another child, he may be jolted out of his narrow focus on his desire. The "jolt" may make the child aware of the other's desire, particularly if accompanied by teacher intervention. This awareness creates a small opening through which the child has an opportunity to feel a need to coordinate his desire with the other child's. Constructivist teachers want children to experience this process (*equilibration*) of constructing mental relationships that are both emotional and intellectual during conflict resolution.

For example, a child who grabs a ramp section from another child will no doubt experience a negative reaction that may surprise her. If a teacher simply tells the child to return the piece, the child may obey (give in) but experience this merely as the thwarting of a personal desire. She is likely to focus on feeling angry and is unlikely to think about the feelings or rights of the other child. A constructivist teacher mediates the conflict so as to focus both children on the other's desires and on figuring out how they can solve the problem so both are satisfied and leave the conflict with a feeling of resolution.

The following is an example of a conflict resolution with 4-year-old children, mediated by Christina:

> When Christina hears Will shouting, "Give that back!" she goes to them and sits with them so they are facing each other.
>
> **Christina:** I see you both want the same ramp. Can I help?

Will: She took my ramp. I had it first.

Piper: But, I want it.

Christina: Piper, look at Will. How do you think it made him feel when you took his ramp away?

Piper: [looks at Will] Mad.

Christina: Is that right, Will? Do you feel mad? [Will nods]

Christina: How would you feel if Will took a ramp away from you?

Piper: Mad.

Christina: Would it be all right if Will took your ramp away from you?

Piper: No.

Christina: Is there anything you could do so Will wouldn't be mad anymore and you could both have a ramp? [Christina waits]

Will: Piper could have a ramp from the shelf.

Christina: Piper, Will says you could have a ramp from the shelf. Would that work?

Piper nods. Will walks over to the shelf, picks up a ramp section, and hands it to Piper. Piper smiles and takes the ramp section. Both children are satisfied and ready to go back to work on their ramp structures.

Sometimes when teachers use this technique, especially in the beginning, children put their hands over their ears, turn their backs, or even curl up into a fetal position and will not respond. When this happens, the teacher can tell the children she will solve the problem when they are ready to talk.

Children who are really angry when asked "Would it be all right if Will took your ramp away from you?" may respond by saying they don't care. When they do that, the teacher can say, "I don't believe that. I think you would not want anyone to take your ramp." In the situation above, Will and Piper are willing to cooperate because in the sociomoral atmosphere the teacher has created, they feel safe and respected, and they trust their teacher to help them work out their problem in a way that will satisfy them both.

When teachers devote considerable time to this process of conflict resolution by helping solve many problems in the beginning of the year, after several months many children will be solving interpersonal problems independently. In this way, self-regulation is gradually constructed through many small experiences over a long period of time, even a lifetime.

*   *   *

Children's unique work with materials can inspire teachers to construct their own personal meanings for these ten principles, even going beyond to elaborate these and invent others. We have seen many teachers take these principles, work with the children in their program, and together think of new and wonderful ideas we never would have imagined.

30

5

The Story of Nani

(Or, a Case Where Ramps & Pathways Made a Difference)

One child's transformation, as a result of one teacher's application of the principles described in this book, made a powerful impression on all of us at Freeburg School.

Nani was a very quiet, passive first-grader who lagged significantly in all academic areas. Special education support staff suggested Nani might never progress academically. Her teacher, Beth Van Meeteren, decided to work with Nani more specifically on physical-knowledge activities. Beth was shocked to find that Nani's ramp structures were nothing more than copies of other children's structures and that she did not understand the mental relationships involved:

> Beth places a ramp section on the floor with a marble on it and asks Nani what she would have to do to make the marble roll down the path. Nani does not answer. Probing, Beth places the ramp in Nani's hands, each hand cupping an end. Beth places a marble in the middle of the ramp and asks, "What can you do to get the marble to roll to this end?" Answering with action, Nani begins to raise the ramp above her head, carefully keeping it horizontal.

In Nani's reasoning, the height of the entire horizontal ramp section made the marble move. She had not made the mental relationship between slope and movement of the marble.

> Noticing the marble is staying in the middle, Nani begins to bring the ramp down. In the process, she inadvertently lowers one end, and the marble rolls to the left. Beth asks, "Oh, what happened? How did you get it to roll there?" Nani shrugs. "Is there a way to get the marble to roll to the other end?" Again, Nani begins to raise the ramp above her head, carefully keeping it horizontal. Beth says, "It's not rolling. What is keeping it from rolling?" Nani does not respond. Beth then places her hands over Nani's, gently lifts the left end, and the marble rolls to the right. "What happened? What made it move?" Nani sits for a moment and once again raises the whole ramp.

Again and again, Nani and Beth experimented with rolling the marble on the ramp in Nani's hands until Nani could describe that when she lifted one end higher, the marble would go down to the other side.

With the teacher's guidance, Nani began building simple ramps such as the one shown in Photograph 31, and she began describing how she was making the marble roll. Later, as shown in Photograph 32, Nani built ramps and pathways with corners and more sections. Finally, she was able to build a more complex ramp within a confined area (Photograph 33).

Nani progressed academically. By the end of second grade, Nani's reasoning (mental relationships) demonstrated a growing intelligence. Her performance in reading and mathematics improved. She began to reason about number by adding "unfriendly numbers" to get "friendlier numbers" (e.g., when adding $7 + 5 + 3$, she added $7 + 3$ to make a 10 that adds more easily to 5). She also made a relationship between adding doubles and a closely related fact (e.g., if $6 + 6 = 12$, then $6 + 7$ will be 13 because 7 is one more than 6, and 13 is one more than 12).

Before her intensive work with ramps and pathways, Nani was unable to comprehend even literal information from a short story or connect the story with

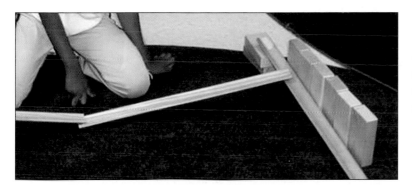

31
As Nani built simple ramps, she was also able to describe how she was making the marble roll.

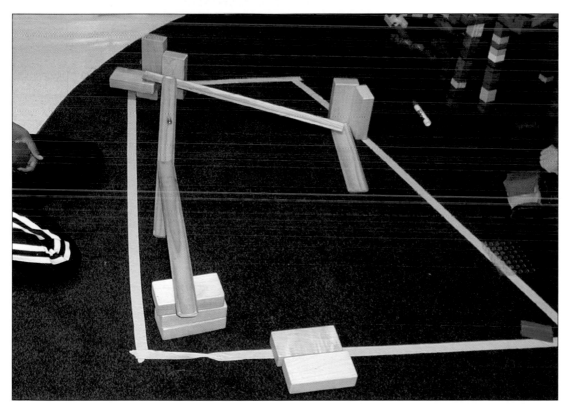

32
Later she built ramps and pathways with corners.

33
Eventually, Nani was able to build a more complex ramp structure within a confined area.

events or experiences in her own life. After constructing mental relationships in physical-knowledge activities, Nani began to reason about what was happening in stories, often reflecting on the illustrations. For example:

> In one session, Nani comments on an illustration in the book she is reading. She notices the glare of the sun on the top of an iceberg. Beth probes by asking, "The sun isn't on this page. If we could make the page bigger to see the sun, where would the sun be?" Nani points to the correct side. "How do you know?" "Because it's shining on this side of the iceberg. Besides, look at the shadows of the penguins. The sun has to be there for the shadows to be on that side."

Thus, Nani had constructed and coordinated spatial relationships among object, light source, and shadow.

Although we cannot prove that Nani's enhanced reasoning in literacy and mathematics is a result of her work with physical-knowledge activities, her seemingly miraculous progress did not occur until after she constructed correct mental relationships in physical-knowledge activities.

Note: Her progress is consistent with Kamii's (Kamii, Rummelsburg, & Kari 2005) research on the positive effects of physical-knowledge activities on arithmetic test results and with the theoretical notion that mental relationships develop over the course of physical-knowledge activities.

References

Bredekamp, S., ed. 1987. *Developmentally appropriate practice in early childhood programs serving children from birth through age 8.* Expanded edition. Washington, DC: NAEYC.

Bredekamp, S., & C. Copple, eds. 1997. *Developmentally appropriate practice in early childhood programs.* Rev ed. Washington, DC: NAEYC.

Developmental Studies Center. 1996. *Ways we want our class to be: Class meetings that build commitment to kindness and learning.* Oakland, CA: Author.

DeVries, R. 1986. Children's conceptions of shadow phenomena. *Genetic, Social, and General Psychology Monographs* 112 (4): 479–530.

DeVries, R., & L. Kohlberg. 1987/1990. *Constructivist early education: Overview and comparison with other programs.* Washington, DC: NAEYC.

DeVries, R., & B. Zan. 1994. *Moral classrooms, moral children: Creating a constructivist atmosphere in early education.* New York: Teachers College Press.

DeVries, R., & B. Zan. 1995. Creating a constructivist classroom atmosphere. *Young Children* 51 (1): 4–13.

DeVries, R., B. Zan, C. Hildebrandt, R. Edmiaston, & C. Sales. 2002. *Developing constructivist early childhood curriculum: Practical principles and activities.* New York: Teachers College Press.

Dewey, J. 1913/1975. *Interest and effort in education.* Edwardsville, IL: Southern Illinois Press.

Duckworth, E. 2006. *"The having of wonderful ideas" and other essays on teaching and learning.* 3d ed. New York: Teachers College Press.

Edmiaston, R. 2002. Assessing and documenting learning in constructivist classrooms. In *Developing constructivist early childhood curriculum: Practical principles and activities*, eds. R. DeVries, B. Zan, C. Hildebrandt, R. Edmiaston, & C. Sales, 53–67. New York: Teachers College Press.

Edwards, C., L. Gandini, & G. Forman. 1998. *The hundred languages of children: The Reggio Emilia approach—Advanced reflections.* 2d ed. Westport, CT: Albex.

Evans, R.I. 1973. *Jean Piaget: The man and his ideas.* New York: Dutton.

Gilbert, L. 1984. *I can do it! I can do it! 135 successful independent learning activities.* Mt. Rainer, MD: Gryphon House.

Helm, J.H., & S. Beneke. 2003. *The power of projects: Meeting contemporary challenges in early childhood classrooms—Strategies & solutions.* New York: Teachers College Press; and Washington, DC: NAEYC.

Helm, J.H., & L. Katz. 2011. *Young investigators: The project approach in the early years.* 2d ed. New York: Teachers College Press; and Washington, DC: NAEYC.

Howes, C., & S. Ritchie. 2002. *A matter of trust: Connecting teachers and learners in the early childhood classroom.* New York: Teachers College Press.

Jones, E., & G. Reynolds. 1992. *The play's the thing: Teachers' roles in children's plays.* New York: Teachers College Press.

Kamii, C., & R. DeVries. 1978/1993. *Physical knowledge in preschool education: Implications of Piaget's theory.* New York: Teachers College Press.

Kamii, C., J. Rummelsburg, & A. Kari. 2005. Teaching arithmetic to low-performing, low-SES first-graders. *Journal of Mathematical Behavior* 24 (1): 39–50.

Katz, L.G., & S.C. Chard. 2000. *Engaging children's minds: The project approach.* 2d ed. Stamford, CT: Ablex.

Piaget, J. 1928/1995. *Sociological studies.* L. Smith, ed. New York: Routledge. (Original works published 1928–1964)

Piaget, J. 1932/1965. *The moral judgment of the child.* New York: Free Press.

Piaget, J. 1941/1952. *The child's conception of number.* New York: Norton.

Piaget, J. 1948/1973. *To understand is to invent.* New York: Grossman.

Piaget, J. 1952. *The origins of intelligence in children.* New York: International Universities Press.

Piaget, J. 1954/1981. *Intelligence and affectivity: Their relationship during child development.* Berkeley: University of California Press.

Piaget, J. 1964. Development and learning. In *Piaget rediscovered: A report of the Conference on Cognitive Studies and Curriculum Development*, eds. R.E. Ripple & V.N. Rockcastle, 7–20. Ithaca, NY: Cornell University Press.

Piaget, J. 1969/1970. *Science of education and the psychology of the child.* New York: Viking Compass.

Piaget, J. 1971/1974. *Understanding causality.* New York: Norton.

Piaget, J. 1973. Piaget takes a teacher's look. *Learning: The magazine for creative teaching* 2 (2): 22–27.

Piaget, J. 1974/1976. *The grasp of consciousness: Action and concept in the young child.* Cambridge, MA: Harvard University Press.

Piaget, J. 1975/1985. *The equilibration of cognitive structures: The central problem of intellectual development.* Chicago: University of Chicago Press.

Piaget, J., & R. Garcia. 1983/1989. *Psychogenesis and the history of science.* New York: Columbia University Press.

Piaget, J., & B. Inhelder. 1948/1956. *The child's conception of space.* New York: Norton.

Watson, M., & L. Ecken. 2003. *Learning to trust: Transforming difficult elementary classrooms through developmental discipline.* San Francisco: Jossey-Bass.

Index